MAKING GLASS BEADS

MAKING GLASS BEADS

CINDY JENKINS

Lark Books
A Division of Sterling
Publishing Co., Inc.
New York

Editor: Leslie Dierks
Art Director: Kathy Holmes
Photography: As noted; all how-to photography by Evan Bracken
Illustrations: Orrin Lundgren
Production: Elaine Thompson, Kathy Holmes

Library of Congress has cataloged the hardcover edition as follows:
Jenkins, Cindy, 1953–
    Making glass beads / Cindy Jenkins.
      p. cm.
    Includes index.
    ISBN 1-887374-16-7
    1. Glass blowing and working. 2. Glass beads. I. Title.
TT298.J46   1997
748.8'5--dc21   96-49598
                               CIP

10 9 8 7 6 5 4 3 2

Published by Lark Books, a division of
Sterling Publishing Co., Inc.
387 Park Avenue South, New York, N.Y. 10016

First Paperback Edition 2004
© 1997 by Cindy Jenkins

Distributed in Canada by Sterling Publishing
c/o Canadian Manda Group, 165 Dufferin Street
Toronto, Ontario, Canada M6K 3H6

Distributed in the U.K. by Guild of Master Craftsman Publications Ltd.
Castle Place, 166 High Street, Lewes, East Sussex, England BN7 1XU
Tel: (+ 44) 1273 477374, Fax: (+ 44) 1273 478606
Email: pubs@thegmcgroup.com, Web: www.gmcpublications.com

Distributed in Australia by Capricorn Link (Australia) Pty Ltd.
P.O. Box 704, Windsor, NSW 2756 Australia

If you have questions or comments about this book, please contact:
Lark Books, 67 Broadway, Asheville, NC 28801, (828) 253-0467

Manufactured in China

ISBN 1-887374-16-7 (hardcover) 1-57990-633-8 (paperback)

For information about custom editions, special sales, premium and corporate purchases, please contact Sterling Special Sales Department at 800-805-5489 or specialsales@sterlingpub.com

C O N T E N T S

Top: Al Janelle, red gumball, 3.2 x 2.2 cm; topaz light bulb, 3.8 x 2.1 cm
Photograph: Al Janelle

Bottom: Angela Green (left), *Red Rose Bead*, heavily cased, 2.8 x 2.5 cm; Char Eagleton, two heavily cased daffodil beads, 3.1 x 2 cm (larger)
Photograph: Evan Bracken

Opposite top: Lorraine Yamaguchi, patterned dichroic bead, 2.5 x 1.6 cm
Photograph: Evan Bracken

Opposite center: Al Janelle, assortment of twisties
Photograph: Al Janelle

Opposite bottom: Bernadette Fuentes, trio of calla lily beads with poked and cased dots, 2 x 3 cm
Photograph: Tommy Elder

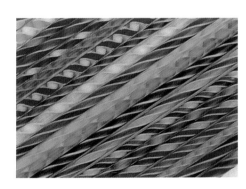

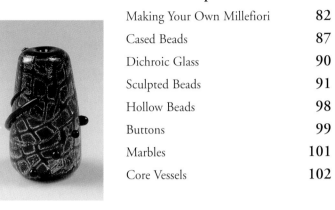

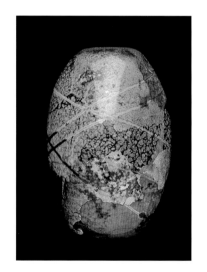

Top left: Tom Holland, triple-strand necklace of beads decorated with gold leaf, 3.8 x .8 cm (largest)

Photograph: Tom Holland

Top right: Patricia Frantz (left), bicone with light casing at ends and heavy casing around center, 3.8 x 1.7 cm; Alice Foster-Zimmerman (right), cylinder with flattened casing around center, 4.2 x 2.3 cm

Photograph: Evan Bracken

Center: René Roberts, *Moss Series*, gold leaf, 3.2 x 1.6 cm

Photograph: George Post

Bottom: Kristina Logan, "ivory" beads with dots, 1.3 x 5.1 cm (disk)

Photograph: Dean Powel

INTRODUCTION

For MANY YEARS I hardly thought about beads, except as something my Grandma and aunts wore. Then a good friend invited me to go to a gem and jewelry show with her. I thought it sounded interesting and said "yes." I dragged my reluctant (and much less interested) husband along, and as my friend patiently pointed out little subtleties of the different beads, I started really looking at them. By the end of the day I was totally enthralled with beads and much poorer. My husband was just as bad, making sure I saw any beads he thought I hadn't noticed and adding his own selections to our growing pile.

Before long I was running wires through beads and soldering them onto my stained glass, dangling them from lamps, using them for shade pulls, attaching them to box handles, and even putting them on my shoelaces. Nothing was safe!

As I continued to collect beads, I started thinking about how they were made. Because I have an extensive background in many different areas of glass working, I began to wonder if I could make my own glass beads. That thought started me in a direction that eventually changed the course of my life. I began to experiment with materials I had on hand, took any classes I could find, and talked to anyone I thought might know something about beads and how they're made. While playing at beadmaking on my own, I discovered that other people were equally fascinated and wanted to learn how to make beads. I eventually started teaching classes, which led to writing an instructional book and then to designing and developing beadmaking tools.

For thousands of years the glass trade was surrounded in secrecy, until Antonio Neri, an Italian glassmaker, published the first book of glassmaking in 1612. Like Neri, I believe in sharing what I know. This book will expose you to a wealth of techniques, tools, and ideas for making your own beads and for making your beads more interesting. As is true with most crafts, there are no hard and fast rules and no right or wrong methods for making glass beads. Don't be afraid to experiment. Try every approach that interests you and let the results point your direction. By copying, combining, and adding to the techniques suggested in this book, your own style will emerge for you to refine and embellish. Even when things don't work out as planned, you can usually learn something. You might even discover a new and exciting approach to beadmaking.

Jana Burnham,
*Asymmetrical Ladder
Necklace*, spiral trails
and dots, 8.9 x 1.3 cm
(largest)

Photograph: Ralph Gabriner

It has been many years since that gem show, and I still love beads as much as ever. I'm always thinking about new ways to make and use them. I also love teaching beadmaking to others. Many of my students have far surpassed my own skills, and that makes me proud of them as well as myself. This book is meant to share my own knowledge and the numerous ideas and techniques I have learned from many generous instructors and beadmakers over the years. Use this book as a guide for starting to make and decorate beads that are beyond your wildest imagination. Make them as beautiful as you can; beads have been known to last thousands of years. Have fun, learn as much as you can, and remember to pass it on to others.

A History of Glass & Glass Beads

Top: Knife, possibly 1400–1800 A.D., possibly Central America, reddish brown obsidian with translucent gray-black inclusions, pressure-flaked all over, 22.8 x 4 cm

Gift of J.J. Klejman, © The Corning Museum of Glass

Bottom: Flask, core-formed, Egypt, New Kingdom, late 18th–19th Dynasty, 1360–1240 B.C., 11.5 cm high

© The Corning Museum of Glass

What Is Glass?

The first glass was formed over 40 million years ago by the tremendous heat and pressure of erupting volcanoes. This naturally occurring substance made of quickly cooled lava is called *obsidian.* Obsidian is usually black, but reds and greens are sometimes found. Thin sections of obsidian look translucent or even transparent.

Man-made glass is another story, and nobody really knows how, when, or where it first came about, but almost everyone agrees it was probably accidental. The raw ingredients of glass (sand, potash, and lime) are common materials found almost everywhere. Today it is believed that the first man-made glass was produced about 3500 B.C. in Anatolia and Mesopotamia.

Glass is a singular material, often imitated, but never equaled. For years no one knew exactly how to classify it. Because no better definition existed, it was often categorized with metals. Glass behaves like a metal in some respects, although it has no definite melting or freezing point. As you heat glass, it becomes more fluid, and as it cools, it becomes increasingly rigid. Glass can be worked as if it were a mineral or gemstone, yet it has no crystalline structure. It is now considered to be a supercooled liquid because of its random atomic structure; at room temperatures, glass is so sluggish that it acts as a solid. Glass is in a class by itself, as well it should be.

Glass varies in translucency from perfectly transparent to completely opaque, and it can be made any color of the rainbow simply by adding differ-

ent metallic oxides to the original melt. Cobalt produces blue, iron and copper create green and turquoise, and many beautiful shades ranging from peach to cranberry are the result of adding gold to the blend. These rosy hues are often called "gold pink" or "gold ruby," although the word "gold" refers to the chemical composition rather than the color of the glass.

Glass is an extremely versatile material. In addition to being poured, molded, stretched, and formed at different temperatures, it can also be cut, polished, etched, and finished much like a stone.

The Development of Glass Beads

Beads are part of every culture, in all areas of the world. They've been used to decorate the human body and just about everything else with which we surround ourselves, including crowns, headdresses, clothing, furniture, buildings, bags, boxes, and graves. In addition to conveying status, beauty, and power to their wearer, beads are considered to be the earliest evidence of mankind's ability to think abstractly. They're also valuable archeological tools. Because the sophistication of bead manufacturing processes are representative of the cultural level and manufacturing skills of the area in which they're found, beads can be used to help date other artifacts present at the same site.

The oldest known beads date back approximately 40,000 years, and it's likely that beads existed even earlier, though they were probably made of materials that didn't last to tell their stories. Easily pierced objects, such as seeds and berries, were surely used as adornments among early peoples. These were gradually replaced by more enduring found objects, such as shells, bones, and rocks with natural holes. Eventually tools were used to create grooves and holes in many types of objects to facilitate the hanging, stringing, and sewing on of ornaments.

THE STRINGING TOGETHER OF MANY BEADS, AS OPPOSED TO WEARING A SINGLE ONE, OCCURRED AT A VERY EARLY DATE (AT LEAST 28,000 B.C.) AND SUGGESTS A DEEP PRIMAL BELIEF THAT "MORE IS BETTER."

(LOIS SHERR DUBIN, *THE HISTORY OF BEADS*, ABRAMS, 1987)

Many thousands of years passed before the secrets of making glass came to light, and the earliest known objects of man-made glass are beads. Due to the limitations of the early technology, beads, amulets, game pieces, and trinkets were the primary items made of glass for many years.

Ancient Egyptians manufactured vast quantities and types of beads, using them to adorn almost any article of clothing and including them with their dead at burial sites. Many of their beads were made of *faience*, a ceramic precursor to glass that was often used to simulate precious stones. The earliest glass objects were exotic rarities that were reserved exclusively for royalty, but glass beads gradually became available to anyone who could afford them in the commercial market. In addition to beads, Egyptian artists produced small vessels by wrapping heated rods

Head or pendant, 5th–3rd century B.C., Punic, Carthage or Syro-Palestinian Coast, core-formed, applied, and tooled, 3.4 x 2.6 cm
© The Corning Museum of Glass

Necklace, eye canes inlaid on wound glass matrix, Iran, said to be from Amlash, 1st half of the 1st millennium B.C., 2 cm high (large bead)
© The Corning Museum of Glass

of glass around preshaped cores made of sand or other materials. While the glass was still molten, a pointed tool was dragged across it to create delicate feathered patterns.

The Hellenistic and Roman eras saw the rise of mosaic glass beads. Also called *millefiori*, or "thousand flowers," these complex designs were constructed by bundling several colored glass rods together into *canes*, which created the desired patterns in cross section. After heating and fusing the glass rods together, a cane was stretched and its pattern miniaturized. Slices cut from a single cane could be used to decorate numerous beads. Glass technology was ultimately mastered to such an extent that intricate portraits and mosaic designs could be incorporated into the surface of even a tiny bead.

In medieval Europe, the trade of glassmaking was closely controlled and passed from father to son. Unless you came from a family of glassmakers, it was extremely difficult to learn anything about the craft. The secrets of glassmaking were and still are jealously guarded in Venice, which became the glass and beadmaking center of the world during the Renaissance. During the late 13th century, the Venetians went so far as to move their entire glassmaking industry to the island of Murano, which effectively quarantined their artisans and secured Venetian dominance of the technology.

The secrecy surrounding the art of glassmaking during this period was reflected by the fact that no books were published on the subject until the early 17th century. Antonio Neri, a glassmaker from Florence, authored *L'Arte Vetraria (The Art of Glass),* which became *the* source book for fine glassmaking for more than 200 years. Written in 1612, it took another 50 years for the book to become available in English.

Although Venice maintained its preeminence for centuries, the Germans, Dutch, and other Europeans also manufactured glass beads, which were carried in quantity by their explorers and trade ships to every continent. Relatively cheap to produce, the beads served as ballast during the voyage and valuable currency at their destination. In America, glass beads were exchanged for furs, tobacco, and sugar; in Africa, they were traded for slaves, ivory, and gold.

The evolution toward greater mass production of beads in modern times was countered early in the 20th century by the influences of the Arts and Crafts movement and Art Nouveau. A return to handcrafts and the incorporation of simple, elegant design into everyday objects were the guiding principles for the Arts and Crafts movement. Art Nouveau was more flamboyant in style but also stressed the importance of design over the preciousness of materials. The joint emphasis on individual creativity and bringing good design within everyone's reach continues to influence beadmakers today.

Glass is no longer a precious commodity, reserved only for the elite, and the technology is no longer a deep, dark secret known only to a few. Today anyone with a few simple tools and materials and a little creative energy can make beautiful glass beads. Fit for royalty, in fact.

GETTING STARTED

Cindy Jenkins, bracelet and assortment of beads, various shapes and decorative techniques

Photograph: courtesy of *Glass Patterns Quarterly*

BASIC TOOLS & SUPPLIES

Because of the growing popularity of glass beads, the materials and equipment for making them are now more readily available than ever before. Many local stained glass stores and bead shops carry beadmaking supplies, and others will special-order them for you. You may find supplies at a local bead show, and there are several suppliers now available on the Internet.

GLASS

Glass used for beadmaking is typically sold in rods about ¼ inch (6 mm) in diameter, although other sizes are also available. Having the glass in rod form makes it easy to roll freely in your hand and shape into beads. Glass rods come in a rainbow of opaque and transparent colors, and filigrana rods have cores of opaque color encased in clear glass. Dichroic glass, available in rods and narrow strips of sheet glass, has a thin, metallic-looking coating that shimmers when angled toward light.

Some glass colors are called *striking* colors. These start out one shade and change to their true color when subjected to the proper heat. Most glass looks as if it's a different color when it's hot (*e.g.*, red, yellow, and orange all appear black when hot), but striking colors permanently change to a new color when sufficient heat is applied.

When choosing glass for your beads, make sure that it's all compatible. Glass that's compatible will expand and contract the same amount during the heating and cooling phases; if beads are made with incompatible glass, they may crack after cooling. You can determine compatibility by referring to the *coefficient of expansion* (COE) for each type of glass you plan to use. The COE is the measure of the rate of expansion of glass as it's heated, and for two or more types of glass to be compatible

Top: Inara Knight, *Spring*, tabular bead decorated with stringer and frit, 4.4 x 3.3 cm

Photograph: Evan Bracken

Center: Barbara Thomas-Yerace, bicones, 2.8 cm long (largest)

Photograph: Evan Bracken

Bottom: Michael Barley, poked and cased floral bead, 2.5 x 2 cm

Photograph: Evan Bracken

Types of glass rod (left to right): filigrana, opalino, transparent, dichroic, opaque

HOT TIP

FOR THOSE OF YOU FAMILIAR WITH THE PROCESS OF GLASS FUSING, YOU MAY USE ¼-INCH TO ⅜-INCH (6 TO 10 MM) STRIPS OF TESTED-COMPATIBLE SHEET GLASS IN PLACE OF RODS. BULLSEYE AND UROBOROS BOTH MANUFACTURE FUSIBLE GLASS, WHICH IS NOW WIDELY AVAILABLE IN A BROAD CONTEMPORARY PALETTE, AND THEIR GLASS IS A SUITABLE ALTERNATIVE TO EFFETRE GLASS ROD.

REMEMBER THAT "TESTED-COMPATIBLE" APPLIES ONLY WITHIN A SINGLE PRODUCT LINE AND NOT BETWEEN MANUFACTURERS, UNLESS SO STATED. TESTED-COMPATIBLE BULLSEYE AND UROBOROS WILL WORK TOGETHER, BUT NEITHER IS COMPATIBLE WITH EFFETRE PRODUCTS. AS OF THIS WRITING, ONLY EFFETRE SHEET GLASS IS COMPATIBLE WITH EFFETRE PRODUCTS.

MOST SHEET GLASS TENDS TO BE A LITTLE STIFFER AND HARDER TO HANDLE FOR TORCH WORK; ROLLING A FLAT STRIP IN YOUR HAND IS A BIT TRICKIER THAN ROLLING A ROUND ROD. FLAT STRIPS OF GLASS ALSO TEND TO HEAT MORE UNEVENLY, MAKING THEM MORE SUSCEPTIBLE TO THERMAL SHOCK AND BREAKAGE.

for beadmaking, they must have COEs within two to three points of each other. (When used for larger work, different types of glass must have COEs within one point.) Generally speaking, the higher the COE, the softer and more workable the glass will be. (See page 108 for more information about COEs and other technical aspects of glass.)

Different types of glass vary with regard to the amount of time and heat they require to soften, bend, and melt. Hard glass, such as Pyrex, requires more time and/or heat to achieve the same effect as soft glass, such as Effetre, Bullseye, or Uroboros.

Lampworkers who make large sculptural objects tend to work with hard glass. Because it expands so much less than soft glass upon heating, hard glass is more forgiving of less-than-even heat, allowing you to join many sections together. Hard glass is also much stronger than soft glass, which makes it a better choice for goblets, bracelets, and sculptures. When learning to make glass beads, start with soft glass, which is designed to melt at a relatively low temperature.

Top: Heather Trimlett, assorted dotted beads, 1.3 x 1.3 cm (typical)

Photograph: Patty Hulet

Bottom: James Smircich, bicolored bead with dots on dots, 2.8 cm high

Photograph: Evan Bracken

Sue Richers Elgar (left), pendant bead with stacked dots, 1.3 x 3.2 cm; Kate Fowle (right), double dots on dots, 1.1 x 2.1 cm

Photograph: Evan Bracken

Jana Burnham, raked squiggle line (left), 1.3 x 2.4 cm; raked stripes (right), 1.9 x 1.7 cm

Photograph: Evan Bracken

TORCH

The most important beadmaking tool is a source of heat for melting glass. Many torch types are available, ranging from small, inexpensive single-fuel torches to sophisticated oxygen-propane systems. A single-fuel torch works with brazing fuel; oxygen-propane systems blend oxygen and propane together to create a burnable mixture.

A single-fuel torch is a good choice for beginners. Its flame isn't as hot as that produced by an oxygen-propane torch, so it allows you more working time to construct your beads. Be sure to purchase a torch that is rated for brazing fuel, which burns hotter than ordinary propane. Among the various single-fuel torches available, one model, the Hot Head, is designed specifically for making glass beads.

An oxygen-propane torch produces a flame that is approximately 1700 to 1900°F (930 to 1040°C) hotter than the flame from a single-fuel torch using brazing fuel. This hotter flame allows you to work much faster. Although the extra speed is sometimes a disadvantage for beginners trying to learn how to work with molten glass, once your skills develop, you can take advantage of that extra heat to work faster and larger.

Oxygen-propane torches come in pre-mix and surface-mix designs. In a pre-mix system, the oxygen and propane are blended together inside the torch and exit together at the tip. Premix systems tend to be noisier and are more prone to backfiring with a loud pop if the flow rate of fuel is too low. With a premix torch you can get a very small pinpoint flame if needed, but the surface-mix system allows much more control over the flame quality. Surface mixing also produces a hotter, quieter flame without backfiring.

When deciding which type of torch to purchase, there are several factors you might consider.

Scale of work: If you plan to make sculptural pieces, goblets, heavy marbles, and very large beads, you should look at oxygen-propane torches that can provide a suitably wide flame. If you're going to concentrate on making beads, either type of system will work well.

Amount of work anticipated: Is this a hobby, or are you planning to produce large quantities of work for sale? Oxygen-propane torches allow you to work faster for increased production.

Available space: A single-fuel system can be set up in a very small space and is portable, in case you want to travel with it or give demonstrations. Oxygen-propane systems require large tanks, which must be secured in a location that is easily accessible for refilling or replacement.

Type of glass: Soft glass can be worked with a single-fuel or oxygen-propane torch. If you plan to work with hard glass, you'll need an oxygen-propane system. Hard glass is considerably stiffer and needs more heat to manipulate.

Price: A single-fuel system is by far the least expensive setup to purchase and use. Many beadmakers start with a smaller system before investing in an oxygen-propane setup.

Local codes: Code restrictions for your studio or workplace may prohibit the use of oxygen tanks. Check your local ordinances before making your investment.

FUEL

Depending on the torch you select, you will need one or more types of fuel to create a proper flame.

Brazing fuel is a modified propane gas or blended fuel that burns hotter and cleaner than ordinary propane, allowing you to work faster and obtain brighter colors in your glass. Brazing fuels are available in one-pound (.5 kg) canisters and in larger, refillable tanks. Propylene, Hi-Intensity Fuel, Apache, Chem-Tane, and MAPP gas are some typical examples of brazing fuels; you may find different brand names in your region, but the tank should say *brazing* somewhere on the label.

Propane is a compressed bottled gas that is used in combination with oxygen to create a very hot flame for bead-making. (It's not desirable to use propane without oxygen because it burns cooler and less completely, resulting in duller colors in your glass.) Propane is widely available in tanks of various sizes.

Natural gas may be used in place of propane, if you have access to it in your area. Have a licensed and quali-fied plumber attach the fittings to your gas line to meet local codes.

Oxygen isn't actually a fuel; it's an accelerant that aids combustion. Used in combination with propane or natural gas, it creates a much hotter flame.

REGULATORS

Propane and oxygen are compressed into their tanks at pressures far too high for direct use. To manage the flow of gas, a regulator is attached to each tank at the hose connection. The regulator's automatic valve lowers the pressure of the gas to a suitable level as it exits the tank and flows into the hose.

There are two types of regulators: single- and two-stage. A single-stage regulator reduces the high pressure of the tank to a suitable working pressure in one step. With a single-stage regulator,

Top: Michael Barley, stratified dots, 2.9 x 3 cm

Photograph: Evan Bracken

Center: Char Eagleton, *Gram's Graniteware,* sculptural bead enhanced with frit, 3.3 cm high

Photograph: Evan Bracken

Bottom: Patricia Sage, *Tiger Eye Bead,* stringer decoration and raked dot, 5.1 x 3.8 cm

Photograph: Tom Holland

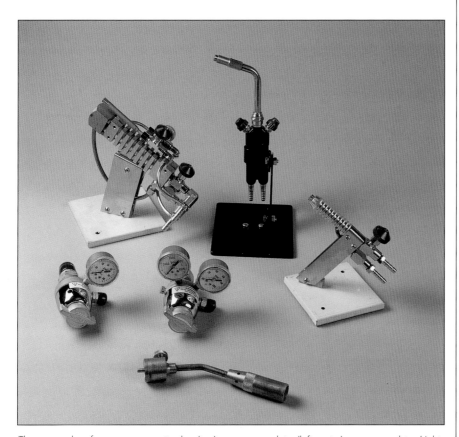

Three examples of oxygen-propane torches (top), propane regulator (left center), oxygen regulator (right center), single-fuel torch (bottom)

the flame can fluctuate as the tank empties and the pressure drops. You may need to make periodic adjustments to maintain the steady pressure required for a consistent flame. A two-stage regulator maintains a constant flow by reducing pressure in two steps. In the first stage, the pressure is reduced by a fixed amount. The gas from this chamber then feeds into a second stage, where it is adjustable down to the desired working pressure. Because they have more complicated mechanisms, two-stage regulators are more expensive than single-stage models.

Fuel regulators have left-handed threads, and oxygen regulators have right-handed threads, so the two can never be attached to the wrong tanks by mistake. Oxygen regulators are considerably stronger than fuel regulators, since oxygen is stored at a much higher pressure.

MANDRELS

Mandrels are stainless steel rods on which beads are constructed. They're available in various thicknesses, and the diameter of the mandrel determines the size of the hole in your bead. The mandrels I commonly use are 9 inches (23 cm) long and ³⁄₃₂ inch (2.4 mm) thick. Using a narrower steel rod will give you a smaller hole in your bead, but thinner mandrels are easier to bend and distort while working and removing beads. A kinked mandrel should be cut off or thrown away. Thicker rods are easier for beginners because they're less susceptible to bending and have a bit more surface area for holding the bead in place.

How you plan to use your beads may be a consideration in selecting your mandrels. For example, if you wish to string your beads on a leather cord, you'll need to make them with bigger mandrels than you might normally use.

BEAD SEPARATOR

This mixture of alumina and high-fire clay provides a buffer between the glass and the steel rod so that the bead can be removed after it cools. Many formulas are available, both in powdered form and in premixed solutions. Sometimes kiln wash or shelf primer is substituted.

FIBER BLANKET

Hot beads taken from the torch and allowed to air-cool are likely to crack because of uneven and overly rapid cooling. Placing your beads between two layers of an insulating blanket made of nonasbestos ceramic fibers will allow them to cool more slowly and be less prone to breakage. Two pieces, each approximately 6 by 12 by 1 inch (15 x 30.5 x 2.5 cm), work well.

As an alternative, you can use vermiculite heated in a slow cooker, electric skillet, or pot kept warm on a hot plate. There should be a sufficient volume of vermiculite in the pot to provide substantial insulation to all the beads you plan to make in one sitting.

BEAD RAKE

This is a hooked metal instrument, resembling a dental probe, that is used for manipulating the hot surface of your glass bead to create more design possibilities.

MARVER

A marver is any smooth, heat-proof surface used to roll or press your hot bead for shaping. It is generally made of graphite or metal, such as aluminum or steel. For more design possibilities, consider using a dual-action marver—a marver that is smooth on one side and grooved on the other. The grooves are a great way to introduce a surface texture to your hot glass.

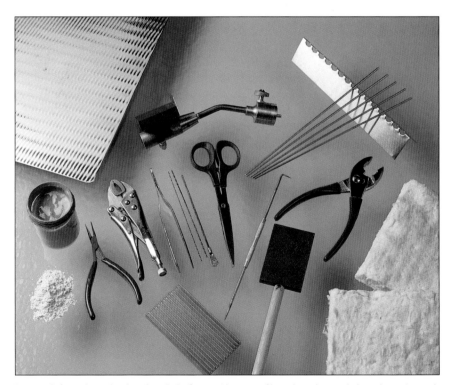

Basic tools for making glass beads include (first row) heat-proof board, torch, mandrels, rod rest, (second row) premixed bead separator, vise-grip pliers, large tweezers, bead core scrapers, scissors, bead rake, slip-joint pliers, (third row) powdered kiln wash, needle-nose pliers, grooved marver, graphite paddle, fiber blanket.

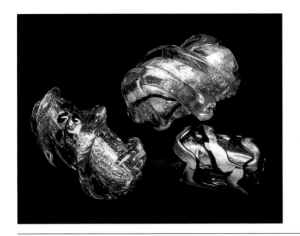

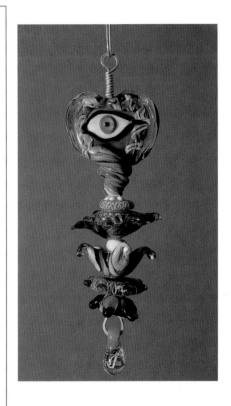

A torch marver is a graphite block mounted on a stainless steel base that is easily attached to your torch head, making an excellent surface for pre-heating cold glass or shaping hot beads. Additionally, because this tool is heated by the torch head, it doesn't chill your bead as quickly as a separate marver does, allowing you to spend more time shaping the hot glass. Torch designs vary in how much heat they transfer to an attached marver.

GRAPHITE PADDLE
This handy tool consists of a small, flat piece of graphite with smooth sides and a wooden handle. Like a marver, it's used for shaping your beads, but a graphite paddle is easier to pick up and maneuver because of its handle. Graphite is a very slick, slippery surface for hot glass, and you'll find the glass rolls very smoothly over it.

FLATTENERS
This tool, which resembles a pair of large tweezers but has flat plates welded onto the tips, is used to squeeze hot glass and flatten beads. Flatteners are available in various sizes.

ROD REST
This grooved metal shelf prevents your glass rods from rolling around on your work surface and keeps the hot ends pointed away from you, while slightly elevating them for more even cooling. Using a rod rest also prevents the hot ends from picking up debris from your work surface.

HEAT-PROOF BOARD
If you don't have a metal or other non-flammable surface on your work bench, a heat-proof board is strongly recommended. This will prevent any damage to your work surface from small pieces of hot glass dropping onto it.

MISCELLANEOUS HAND TOOLS
For pinching and pulling hot glass into desired shapes, a pair of stainless steel or carbon steel tweezers makes an invaluable tool. Make sure the tweezers are at least 4 inches (10 cm) long, and consider investing in both blunt and sharp-tipped models for achieving different effects.

Regular slip-joint pliers are useful for grasping the mandrel when removing a cooled bead, but vise-grip pliers are even better. Needle-nose pliers are handy for pinching and shaping hot glass.

A sharp pair of scissors with thin blades and small tips can be used to snip hot glass.

To brush scraps of glass and debris from your tools and work surface, keep a small bench brush handy.

Top left: Pati Walton, dichroic beads, 5.1 cm long (largest)
Photograph: Mike Bush

Top right: Kristen Frantzen Orr, five floral plunge beads, 2.2 cm dia. (largest)
Photograph: Jeff Scovil

Bottom: Patricia Sage, *Sacred Eye*, 15.2 x 5.1 cm
Photograph: Darol Strieb

Far left: Michael Max, raked stratified dots, 3 x 4.6 cm

Photograph: Evan Bracken

Left: Sue Richers Elgar, two dinosaur beads with twistie decorations, 4 cm long

Photograph: Evan Bracken

SPECIALIZED TOOLS

Once you become experienced with beadmaking and want to create specialized effects more easily, you may want to add some of these tools to your collection.

Pin vise: A metal handle with an adjustable collet that tightens the vise at one end. Some beadmakers like to insert short mandrels into pin vises to give them more substantial handles to grasp.

Tungsten pick: A pointed tungsten rod, available in several diameters, this tool can be used for raking or poking.

When heated red-hot, it can be pushed through hot glass to create a clean hole.

Rod nipper: A tool used to bite off small slices of glass from the end of glass rods. It's most often used to cut slices from millefiori rods.

Graphite shaping paddle: A variety of machined shapes are available for all sorts of specific sculpting and shaping applications.

Marble-molding paddle: This tool has varying sizes of machined half-round wells that are used for shaping buttons, marbles, and beads.

Optic mold: This is a small aluminum

mold that has a simple design, such as a heart or star, cut through from top to bottom. The design tapers in diameter, becoming smaller at the bottom than at the top.

Pattern-impressing pliers: Pliers with different designs machined into metal plates, which are welded to the jaws of the pliers. Squeezing hot glass between the plates leaves a specific design embossed in the glass.

Holding fingers: A tool with three to eight fingers, it can be adjusted to different diameters for gripping the exterior of hot glass objects, such as marbles, allowing you to do fire-polishing and other finishing touches.

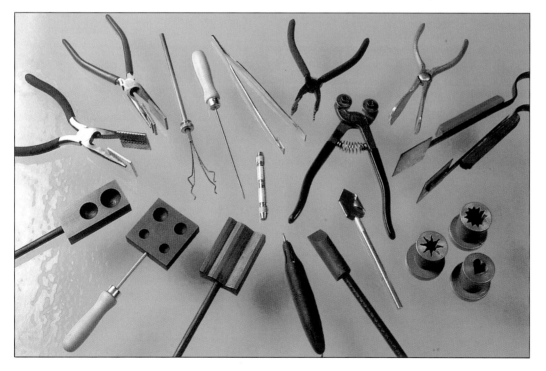

Specialized tools include (clockwise, starting at far left) two examples of pattern-impressing pliers, holding fingers, tungsten pick, pin vise, small flatteners, pattern-impressing pliers, rod nipper, medium flatteners, large flatteners, optic molds, shaping tool, graphite shaping paddle, engraving pen, graphite shaping paddle, two sizes of marble-molding paddles.

Right: Tom Holland, *Warring States Interpretation,* eye beads, 1.8 x 1.5 cm (typical)

Photograph: Tom Holland

Far right: James Smircich, line patterns, 5.2 cm long

Photograph: Evan Bracken

Kiln: Also called an annealer, this is an insulated hot-box used for slowly cooling beads to remove internal stresses that may cause cracking. Kilns are available in a variety of sizes and designs. If portability is a factor, those insulated with fiber are lighter in weight and more compact than those insulated with brick. Fiber insulation allows rapid heat-up, but also rapid cooling. You may need to "fire down" during the cooling cycle by gradually turning the controller to lower settings, or you can purchase an electronic controller to slow the cooling process. A brick-insulated kiln takes longer to heat up and cool down, making a controller less necessary for small objects, such as beads.

Kiln controller: An electronic device that monitors and maintains your kiln at a specific temperature. Designs range from simple to highly sophisticated.

Engraving pen: A tool with a diamond bit that spins at high speed for surface embellishment of beads.

SETTING UP A WORK STATION

When deciding where you want to do your beadmaking, here are some general guidelines for choosing an appropriate location.

- The torch placement should allow for good ventilation without compromising your flame. (Don't work directly in front of the window you plan to open for ventilation.) Ideally your room should have cross ventilation.

- Assess the room for fire safety and any potential fire-related hazards (carpeting on the floor, nearby curtains, stored newspapers or paint); then devise a solution for each (removal, cover-up, etc.)

- Think about what you would do in the event of a problem. Are things arranged in such a way that you can easily reach your fire extinguisher when you need it? Can you quickly get to a telephone or an exit?

LAYOUT OF THE WORK BENCH

First and foremost you will need a sturdy work bench or table. I like one that is high enough for me to stand or sit and work comfortably. If you make beads for long periods of time, it's imperative that your work bench conform to your height, even if it means

Portable kiln (annealer) with fiber insulation and temperature controller

doing some customizing. To make my bench the correct height, I had to raise it 7 inches (18 cm), which allowed me to add a handy storage shelf underneath the work surface.

Plan the arrangement of your supplies and equipment on your work surface so that you never have to reach over or under your torch for tools, mandrels, or glass. A right-handed station will look very different from a left-handed one.

No matter which hand is dominant, your torch belongs directly in front of you, in the center of the nearest edge of your bench. The torch must be fastened securely to the bench so that it can't be knocked over or pulled off if a hose is accidentally yanked. All the tools you normally use with your left hand should stay on the left half of your bench, right-handed tools on the right. It may take some practice before you decide on the exact tool placement that feels most comfortable.

SETTING UP A SINGLE-FUEL TORCH

To set up a single-fuel torch, first firmly screw the torch head onto the disposable tank of brazing fuel. Next fasten a steel L-bracket near the top of the tank with a hose clamp so that the L-bracket and torch head are facing the same direction. Now you can use a C-clamp to secure your torch head to your work bench. Alternately, the L-bracket can be fastened directly to your bench with screws. This setup allows you to adjust your torch and tank to a comfortable height, as well as make it tip-proof. It's very important that your torch be firmly secured while in use.

A typical single-fuel work station with refillable fuel tank. The tools and supplies are arranged for right-handed working.

Opposite left: Char Eagleton, *Kitty Teapot Necklace*, dotted beads with sculptural accent beads, 1 x 1.2 cm (largest round bead), 3.8 cm high (kitty pendant)

Photograph: Evan Bracken

Opposite right: Inara Knight, *Earthstone Necklace*, dichroic glass with frit and stringer decoration, 3.1 cm long (typical larger bead)

Photograph: Evan Bracken

Try to position the torch so that your arms are in a comfortable, relaxed position while you work—you may find yourself making beads for several hours at a time! To determine the most comfortable overall position, experiment by standing and sitting while you work. Padded arm rests are great to prevent fatigue, or try the elbow pads available at sporting goods supply stores.

HOT TIP

IF YOU PLAN TO WORK FOR MORE THAN 30 TO 45 MINUTES, IT'S A GOOD IDEA TO HAVE A SECOND TANK OF FUEL AVAILABLE. ALTHOUGH A FULL 1-POUND (.5 KG) DISPOSABLE TANK SHOULD LAST 4 TO 5 HOURS, WHEN IT'S USED CONTINUOUSLY FOR MORE THAN 30 TO 45 MINUTES, THE CONDENSATION OF GAS VAPORS COOLS THE TANK AND LOWERS THE PRESSURE. ONE WAY TO AVOID THIS PROBLEM IS TO SWITCH TANKS PERIODICALLY. ANOTHER OPTION IS TO WARM THE COLD BOTTOM OF THE TANK IN A CONTAINER OF HOT WATER.

After placing the heat-proof board in front of your torch, scan the area for any flammable items and remove them. Position the insulating blanket in a convenient location on your work bench.

If you find that you're going through a lot of disposable fuel tanks, it will be much cheaper in the long run to invest in a larger, refillable tank. After the initial investment, which may be greater than for a comparable number of disposable tanks, this is a much cheaper way to buy fuel because you're not purchasing a new tank for every pound (.5 kg) of gas. The cost to refill my 6-pound (2.7 kg) tank is approximately 12 percent of what I would pay for an equivalent number of disposable tanks. Although costs vary from region to region, buying fuel for larger, refillable tanks is always much cheaper than purchasing single-use cylinders.

If you decide to use a refillable tank, you will need a hose with adapter fittings because your torch head will not screw directly onto a larger tank. One end of the hose requires a Coleman-type fitting to attach to the torch, and the other end needs a bulk tank fitting. Most propane suppliers can prepare such a hose for you inexpensively. Be sure to tell them you're working with brazing fuel so that you get the appropriate type of hose.

Top: Brian Kerkvliet, vase with twistie base and lip, 3.4 cm high; Barbara Thomas-Yerace, two tiger beads, 1.8 x 2 cm

Photograph: Evan Bracken

Center: Gina Lambert, multicolored bottle beads, 2.3 x 1.5 cm (typical)

Photograph: Evan Bracken

Bottom: Kimberley Adams (top), two disks with simple dots, 2 x 2.8 cm (larger); Barbara Thomas-Yerace (bottom), disk with eye stalks, 2.4 x 3.1 cm

Photograph: Evan Bracken

Heather Trimlett, assorted beads decorated with stringer, 3.8 cm high (teapot)

Photograph: Patty Hulet

Fasten the torch head to the hose and the hose to the tank. After you've screwed the parts together, check both joints for leaks with dish soap slightly diluted with water. This can be done by brushing or spraying a solution of soapy water onto the joints, turning on the tank valve, and opening the torch valve. If bubbles appear, there is gas leaking, and the joints must be screwed together more tightly. If tightening the joints doesn't resolve the leak, try wrapping the threads of the male adapter with Teflon tape (a plumbing/welding supply item). If the hose itself is leaking, it must be taken back to your supplier and repaired or replaced.

A regulator isn't an absolute necessity for a refillable tank system; however, if you're working with a large tank (30 to 60 pounds/13.6 to 27.2 kg), a regulator allows you to adjust your flame precisely, and it keeps the flame at the same intensity throughout your bead-making session. If you add a regulator, you will have three parts to screw together and three joints to check for leaks, but it's still a fairly simple procedure. You'll have to play a little before deciding what pressure works best for you. Be sure to get advice from your gas supplier about what type of regulator, if any, is best for your situation.

OXYGEN-PROPANE SETUP

An oxygen-propane system consists of both an oxygen and a propane tank, each with its own regulator. Both tanks must be connected to the torch through regulators with hoses and proper fittings. The regulators allow you to adjust the levels of fuel and oxygen pressure available to the torch.

You will need to experiment with different settings to find the pressures and fuel mixture that are most comfortable for you. Most lampworkers set the pressure of their oxygen somewhere between 5 and 15 pounds per square inch (psi) and their propane between 1 and 5 psi.

Assembling an oxygen-propane setup should really be done with the help and advice of an expert until you feel comfortable setting up and using all of the components. Have your supplier or

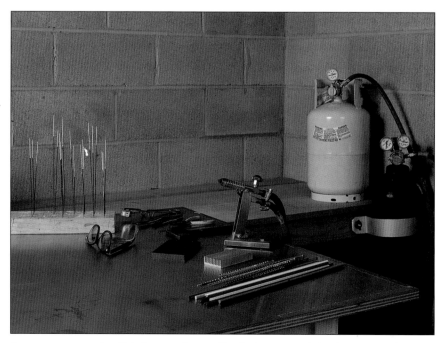

An oxygen-propane setup. Note the green tape marking the hose connected to the oxygen tank.

Above: Lavana Shurtliff, stacked dots, 1.5 x 1.9 cm

Photograph: Evan Bracken

Right: Patricia Sage, *Universal Symbols*, surface manipulation applied to beads of various shapes, 3.8 x 1.9 cm (typical)

Photograph: Tom Holland

an experienced instructor walk you through the process of connecting your tanks, hoses, and regulators so that it's very familiar and you can do everything yourself. You will need to know how to change tanks, check for leaks, and seal those leaks when you find them.

To avoid any confusion, use a green hose to connect the oxygen to the torch and a red one for the propane. If your supplier doesn't have both colors available, mark both ends of one hose with tape to differentiate it from the other. In addition, marking all connectors and handles with an arrow will speed the process of turning the system on and off.

Your oxygen and propane tanks should be chained, preferably outside of your studio, or otherwise secured so that they can't be accidentally knocked over.

No oil should ever be allowed near oxygen tanks; even oil from your fingers on the connections can cause spontaneous combustion. Teflon tape should be used to keep the connections from leaking.

Check-valves (one-way valves) or flash-back arrestors on both regulators are a good idea (I think they're a necessity!) to prevent gas from flowing in the wrong direction. This prevents the flame from burning back into your hoses and tanks, causing damage and a possible explosion. Flashback arrestors have the added feature of a flame quencher to prevent damage to the hoses.

Be sure to keep an up-to-date fire extinguisher on hand.

SAFETY TIPS

EYE PROTECTION

Care should be taken when placing cold glass into a hot flame; if you introduce a rod into the flame too quickly, small pieces of glass may snap off. Always wear eye protection to shield yourself against these potentially hazardous projectiles. Ideally, your glasses should have wraparound temple guards.

Beyond the obvious hazards of broken glass, many beadmakers and other lampworkers are concerned about the potential risks of exposing their eyes to the intense light generated by molten

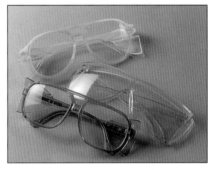

Protect your eyes with safety glasses whenever you're working with glass.

glass in an open flame. According to an evaluation done by the National Institute for Occupational Safety and Health (NIOSH), the amount of infrared and ultraviolet light emitted by hot glass in a flame is insignificant and not considered hazardous. In the range of visible light, hot glass in a flame emits a bright orange-yellow light called the *soda flare*. NIOSH found that although soda flare can be annoying and distracting, it's harmless. Individuals do vary in their sensitivity to this exposure, however, and people need to pay attention to their own reactions to determine if they should take any precautions.

Soda flare can block your ability to see what you're doing, especially with an

Far left: James Smircich, blue bubble bead, 4.1 x 3.1 cm

Photograph: Evan Bracken

Left: Audrie Wiesenfelder, *Leaf Pendant Beads*, pinched beads decorated with silver wire, 5 x 2.4 cm (largest)

Photograph: Tom Van Eynde

oxygen-propane setup, since the intensity of the soda flare is directly related to the temperature of the flame. Many people working with oxygen-propane systems find that they simply cannot see what they're doing without using lenses designed to block soda flare. Most people working with single-fuel systems find that the soda flare is weak enough that it doesn't distract them.

There are currently two eyeglass lens materials available to block soda flare while still allowing you to see what you're doing—*didymium* and *AUR-92*. Didymium lenses were developed in

the 1950s for this specific purpose, and they're very effective at blocking the soda flare while still permitting most of the rest of the visible spectrum to be seen. AUR-92 glass originally was developed to enhance the primary light colors—red, blue, and green—thereby making it easier to judge the temperature of hot glass. Neither didymium nor AUR-92 is necessary with a single-fuel system; either is adequate for an oxygen-propane system. When choosing any pair of safety glasses, make sure that they're not so dark that you run the risk of hurting yourself because you can't see what you're doing!

VENTILATION

When working with an open flame, it is very important to have a well-ventilated work space. Most flames burn incompletely and give off carbon monoxide gas. Carbon monoxide is odorless, invisible, and potentially lethal. The distinctive smell of burning torches is not carbon monoxide but incompletely burnt fuel additives, intended to warn you of increasing exposure. Warning signs of carbon monoxide exposure include headaches, shortness of breath, chest pain, dizziness, fatigue, nausea, and blurred vision.

If you experience any of these symptoms and suspect you've been exposed to carbon monoxide gas, immediately get some fresh air. If you start feeling increasingly ill, seek medical help quickly.

HOT TIP

THE MORE TORCHES YOU HAVE LIT IN A SINGLE ROOM, AND THE LONGER THE TORCHES ARE KEPT ON, THE MORE IMPORTANT VENTILATION BECOMES. INEXPENSIVE CARBON MONOXIDE DETECTORS ARE NOW READILY AVAILABLE AND SHOULD BE A PART OF ANY LAMPWORKER'S STUDIO.

An exhaust fan or backwards fan in a window will help keep fresh air moving in and carbon monoxide moving out. Cross ventilation that doesn't interfere with your flame is ideal, if you have two properly situated windows in or near your studio. This solution is obviously somewhat weather dependent. An ordinary stove ventilation hood placed over your work area and ducted to the outside is another solution.

RESPIRATORY HAZARDS

In addition to carbon monoxide exposure, another respiratory hazard is posed by dust particles you might encounter in your studio. These include powders from the dry bead separator and loose particles of refractory materials, such as vermiculite or ceramic blanket fibers.

HOT TIP

IN JANUARY 1996, NIOSH RELEASED THE RESULTS OF A LANDMARK STUDY OF THE POTENTIAL HEALTH HAZARDS IN A MULTI-USE GLASS STUDIO. A COPY OF THEIR REPORT, HEALTH HAZARD EVALUATION REPORT NO. 95-0119-2554, IS AVAILABLE THROUGH NIOSH AT 4676 COLUMBIA PARKWAY, CINCINNATI, OHIO, 45226, OR BY CALLING 1-800-356-4674.

Take care not to inhale these irritating and potentially harmful dust particles. If necessary, wear a respirator to reduce your exposure. Be particularly aware of hazardous dust that can be stirred up when you're cleaning your studio. To reduce the chances of inhaling particles, moisten any questionable areas or spills with a spray bottle before wiping them with a wet rag.

BURN PREVENTION

Heated objects tend to stay hot for long periods, even after they're no longer glowing. You should treat everything in your bead studio as if it may still be hot and handle things carefully when first picking them up. It's a good idea to have a nearby source of cold water and an aloe plant or aloe gel to deal with minor burns.

Remove any flammable objects from your work area. If you have long hair, keep it tied back.

You need to wear appropriate clothing; jeans, a long-sleeved cotton shirt, and regular shoes will protect you from small annoying burns caused by hot glass fragments. Don't wear polyester, short sleeve shirts, short pants, and open shoes; also avoid loose or rolled-up sleeves, pockets, and pants with cuffs.

GENERAL SAFETY TIPS

• Don't leave your torch unattended.

• Keep small children and animals away from the open torch flame.

• Remember that the torch head remains hot for about fifteen minutes after you've turned off the flame.

• Keep a good, all-purpose fire extinguisher handy in your studio. Make sure it's checked on a regular basis so that it will be in proper working condition should you ever need it.

Kimberley Adams, *Sea-Green Necklace*, spiral trails and dots, 3.8 x 3.2 cm (focal bead)
Photograph: Jerry Anthony

25

Making a Basic Bead

Donna Sauers, basic beads, 1.7 cm (largest)

Photograph: Evan Bracken

PREPARING MANDRELS

The first step in making glass beads is to prepare one or more mandrels. In order to keep the hot glass from permanently adhering to the metal, you must coat each mandrel with a compound called a bead separator. There are several formulations of separators available, both premixed and powdered. One of the most readily available types can be purchased in stores selling stained glass materials. It's called shelf primer or kiln wash and is used for glass fusing. I haven't found much difference between "regular" and "high-temperature" kiln washes, so I recommend using whichever is most available.

If you're using powdered kiln wash as your separator, mix approximately two parts of the powder to one part water. Add the separator to the water and let it sit for a few minutes (slake), until all of the powder sinks into the water. This helps prevent lumps. Now stir until the mixture forms a creamy, yogurtlike consistency. (For this task, a mini-whisk is helpful.) Any extra bead separator mixture can be stored in a screw-cap or snap-lid container, although you may need to add a little water to it the next time you use it.

Many different bead separator formulas are currently available. Some need to air-dry; others can be dried rapidly in the flame. Some separators are more effective at preventing your bead from slipping off the mandrel while you're working, but those same adhesive qualities make it more difficult to remove your bead from the mandrel when you're done. Although some brands leave less residue inside the bead, they're a bit more likely to let your bead pull loose while you're working the hot glass. No separator is perfect, and you may want to compare several to find out which is best for your working style.

To prepare your mandrels to accept the bead separator, rough up one end of each rod with a heavy-duty scrubbing pad or steel wool; then wipe it clean. Dip the prepared end about 2 inches (5 cm) into the separator, giving it a smooth, even coating with no bare spots. Applying the mixture too heavily or in a lumpy fashion will often result in the separator pulling loose while you're making your beads. Overly thick separator is also more likely to crack in the flame.

After dipping your mandrel in the separator, set the rod upright in some sort of stand. I prefer using a wood block that has a gridwork of holes drilled to fit my mandrels, but reasonable alternatives include a block of polystyrene foam, can of sand, or lump of clay.

Allow the coated mandrels to dry thoroughly (about 20 minutes). They will dry from the bottom up, so the tops of the rods will remain dark until they're completely dry. To speed up the drying time, you can set the rods under a light bulb or use a hairdryer. Do not try to dry the mandrels in your torch flame unless your separator is specially formulated for flame-drying. Otherwise, this may cause the separator to bubble and break off.

It's a good idea to prepare about two dozen mandrels so that you don't have to stop constantly while you're working

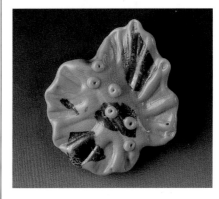

Top: Kimberley Adams, acid-etched tabular bead, 3 x 3 cm
Photograph: Evan Bracken

Center: Kristina Logan, raised dots, 5.1 x 4.1 cm
Photograph: Dean Powel

Bottom: Audrie Wiesenfelder, pinched bead with raised dots, 3.5 x 4.2 cm
Photograph: Evan Bracken

Heather Trimlett, acid-etched beads

Photograph: Patty Hulet

to coat more rods and wait for them to dry. Beadmaking tends to be addictive, so you'll want to be ready to make plenty once you've gotten started. You'll know soon enough how many mandrels to have ready. I've been known to have as many as 100 prepared at one time.

If you're using a flame-dry separator, you won't need to plan ahead or prepare your mandrels in advance. Flame-dry separator is extremely convenient to use; just dip your mandrel and go immediately into the flame to dry!

IGNITING THE TORCH

For a single-fuel system, light your torch by turning the torch valve screw to the left until you hear a slight hiss. Bring a match up to just below the very edge of the torch head so that the gas doesn't extinguish the match.

If the match blows out, turn the gas lower and make sure the match head is just below the rim of the torch head. Another alternative for lighting your torch head is to use a traditional sparker. These tend to be a little more difficult to use than matches—especially for beginners—and may require a bit of practice.

If the flame sputters, turn the gas a bit higher. Once lit, adjust the flame with the valve screw (turn left for more flame, right for less) until you have a nice, sharp blue cone. A bushy or turquoise flame means the fuel is turned up too high.

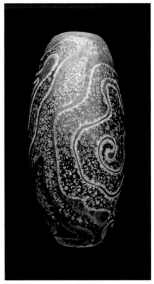

To turn on an oxygen-propane system, first open the valve on your oxygen tank all the way. (This allows the valve to seat and seal properly so that it won't leak.) Set the oxygen pressure by using the regulator valve. Now open the valve on the propane tank, "cracking" it just enough that it can be turned off quickly in case of fire. Again set the gas pressure with the regulator valve.

To ignite the torch, first turn on the propane and light it. Turn up the gas until you have a 6- to 8-inch (15 to 20.5 cm) flame.

Next, slowly turn on the oxygen, gradually increasing it until you have a flame with a ring of small, sharp, blue cones at its base.

Depending on what you're doing and what kind of glass you're using, you may want to use different types of

HOT TIP

AN ALTERNATIVE TO MATCHES IS A FIREPLACE/BARBECUE LIGHTER. BE SURE TO GET A HIGH-QUALITY LIGHTER, THOUGH, AS THE INEXPENSIVE ONES WEAR OUT QUICKLY AND GENERALLY CAN'T BE REFILLED. USE CAUTION WITH THESE LIGHTERS; BECAUSE THEY'RE CONSTRUCTED OF LIGHTWEIGHT PLASTIC, THEY COULD DEVELOP A VERY DANGEROUS FUEL LEAK IF HOT GLASS WERE TO MELT A HOLE IN THEM.

Top left: Liz Ormes, *Scrambles Necklace*, sculptural beads, 1.6 x 7 cm (focal bead)
Photograph: Thomas Ritter

Top right: René Roberts, *Stonework Series*, surface enhanced with metal colorants, 5.1 x 1.6 cm
Photograph: George Post

Bottom: Kristen Frantzen Orr (left), *Water Garden*, heavily cased floral bead, 2. x 2.4 cm; Linda Burnette (top), cased bead with flowers applied to casing, 1.3 x 2.3 cm; Angela Green (right), *Pink Rose*, heavily encased sculptural flower, 3.1 x 1.9 cm
Photograph: Evan Bracken

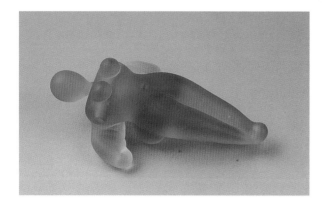

Top left: Sue Richers Elgar, *Angel Goddess*, acid-etched sculptural bead, 6 cm high

Photograph: Evan Bracken

Top right: Ellie Burke, *Catch of the Day*, brooch and earrings, pinched beads, 5.1 x 3.8 cm (brooch)

Photograph: William F. Lemke

Center: Karen Ovington, hollow bead, 3 x 4 cm

Photograph: Tom Van Eynde

Bottom: Inara Knight, dichroic glass tabular beads, 3.3 x 3.5 cm (blue bead at top)

Photograph: Evan Bracken

flames. An oxygen-rich (oxidizing) flame has a tight, sharp cone shape. A fuel-rich flame is called a reduction flame and is larger than an oxidizing flame but cooler and less well defined. Oxidizing flames become hotter as the oxygen flow increases, up to a point. Too much oxygen will start to produce a cooler, sputtering flame and may actually blow out the flame. Generally you will want to work in between these two types, leaning a little more toward an oxidizing flame for soft glass.

When working your glass in the flame, remember to hold it somewhere between the very tip of the blue cone and 1 inch (2.5 cm) above this point. As you move further from the burner tip, the flame's combustion becomes more complete and more oxygen-rich. The inner blue part of the flame consumes all of the oxygen, some of which is needed to keep the colors of your glass from changing.

HOT **TIP**

IF YOUR COLORS ARE MURKY, YOU'RE EITHER WORKING TOO LOW IN THE FLAME OR YOU HAVE THE GAS TURNED UP TOO HIGH. THE FLAME IS ACTUALLY COOLER IF YOU WORK TOO LOW.

FORMING A BEAD

Heat the tip of your glass rod slowly by passing it in and out of the flame to gradually warm it. Be sure to go even more slowly if you're working with filigrana. Since filigrana rods are a combination of two different types of glass—transparent and opaque—they are a bit more susceptible to thermal shock. This is especially so if you're working with an aventurine filigrana; the metal flakes in its core quickly absorb heat and expand against the still-cool outer layer, causing it to break. If the rod keeps popping, try either working higher in the flame or turning down the gas. You can also avoid breakage by preheating the ends, either by leaning them between your torch head and torch marver or by using a hot-plate.

HOT **TIP**

AVENTURINE COMES FROM THE FRENCH WORD *AVENTURE*, MEANING CHANCE. THIS GLASS WAS FIRST MADE IN VENICE IN THE 15TH CENTURY.

Kristen Frantzen Orr, four *Flower Garden* beads, floral plunge, 2.5 cm dia. (largest)

Photograph: Jeff Scovil

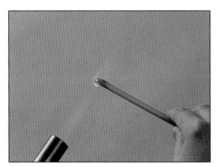

Gradually leave your glass in the flame longer and longer. You'll start to see an orange glow around the rod tip when it's warm enough to remain in the flame continuously. Once you see this glow, you can leave about ¼ to ⅜ inch (6 to 10 mm) of your rod in the flame. When the end of the glass rod starts to glow, begin rotating the glass rod. This keeps the hot glass from sagging and drooping off its center.

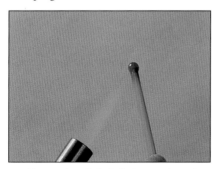

Hold your hand slightly lower than the flame so that the hot end of the rod doesn't stretch. This way the molten glass will thicken and slightly ball up on the end instead of stretching thinner.

When the ball of glass on the end of

your rod has a consistent orange glow all the way through, start heating the coated part of your mandrel. Since mandrels don't need to be warmed gradually, you can put them directly into the flame.

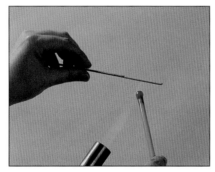

Hold the mandrel in the flame above the glowing glass ball for approximately 10 seconds. At this point you should see a slight incandescent glow. Be sure not to overheat your mandrel, as it doesn't need to be glowing brightly. While heating your mandrel, remember to keep the tip of your glass hot; this takes some practice.

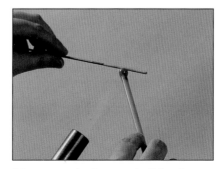

Next, press the front end of the glowing glass ball onto your mandrel in

HOT  **TIP**

AFTER YOU'VE MADE SEVERAL BEADS, YOU'LL PROBABLY FIND THAT YOU HAVE SOME LEFTOVER SHORT LENGTHS OF GLASS RODS OR STRIPS. IF YOU DON'T WANT TO MAKE BEADS BY HOLDING THESE SHORT PIECES IN THE FLAME WITH YOUR PLIERS, YOU CAN FUSE TWO OR MORE TOGETHER TO MAKE LONGER RODS JUST BY MELTING THEIR TIPS IN THE FLAME. ONCE THE HOT ENDS ARE PUSHED FIRMLY TOGETHER, PULL THEM AWAY FROM EACH OTHER UNTIL THE JOINT IS SLIGHTLY THINNER THAN THE ROD DIAMETER. BE CAREFUL; THE JOINT STAYS HOT LONGER THAN YOU MIGHT EXPECT. FUSED RODS CAN BE ALLOWED TO AIR-COOL, BUT BECAUSE THEY HAVEN'T BEEN PROPERLY ANNEALED, YOU MUST TAKE A LITTLE MORE CARE WHEN WARMING THEM IN THE FLAME TO AVOID BREAKAGE.

Top: Inara Knight (left), 2.3 cm long; Kim Adams (center), 2.3 cm long; Inara Knight (right), 2.4 cm long; all acid-etched beads

Photograph: Evan Bracken

Center: James Smircich, *Goddess*, sculptural bead 6.5 cm high

Photograph: Evan Bracken

Bottom: Inara Knight, *Waterfall Pendants*, spot-cased tabular beads, 4.3 x 2.8 cm (larger)

Photograph: Evan Bracken

approximately the middle of the coated portion. At the same time, start rolling the mandrel away from yourself. Remember to stay in the flame during this entire process.

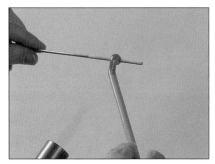

Roll the mandrel until you've wound off as much hot glass as you have available on the end of the glass rod. Once you've wound off all of the molten part of your glass rod, don't try to keep winding into the cold part of the rod. This will force you to start tugging, and the bead may come loose from the mandrel. This can also crack your separator, making the glass permanently stick to your mandrel. If you do run out of hot glass, don't try to force it. Stay in the flame and allow the glass to soften so that you can finish winding off as much glass as you wish. Keep the flame aimed at the cold rod just below the bead.

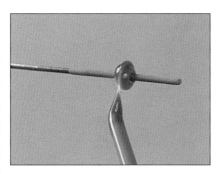

Remember to keep rolling the mandrel away from yourself during wind-off so that you don't create a long string of glass as you pull away. (If you have trouble remembering how to roll *away* from yourself, keep in mind that your thumb should be moving in an upward direction.)

If your bead accidentally works loose from the mandrel, be careful to keep your mandrel horizontal and put it away so that the hot bead doesn't slip down onto your hand.

After you've wound off the molten glass, set the hot glass rod down on the heat-proof work board or your rod rest.

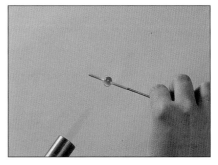

Then switch hands and round up your bead by keeping it in the flame and rotating the mandrel until the bead softens and pulls into a nice round shape. Be sure to keep everything level at this point, as the glass will move in the direction in which you slant it.

Now bring the bead out of the flame and let the glow wear off. Remember to keep the mandrel rotating. As soon as the glow disappears, wave the bead back and forth through the flame several times to even out the heat throughout your bead. When the bead starts to glow slightly, bring it out of the flame and wait a few seconds for the glow to disappear again.

Finally, place the bead, still on its mandrel, between two pieces of 1-inch (2.5 cm) ceramic fiber blanket or in a container of vermiculite. The bead will take

approximately 20 to 30 minutes to cool in the insulating blanket; with vermiculite, the speed of cooling will depend on whether you're using it hot or cold. (Hot vermiculite allows the bead to cool more slowly.) Slow cooling prevents the outside of the bead from cooling faster than its center, which creates stress in the bead and can cause cracking. This step will take a little practice.

Congratulations, you have just made your first bead!

At this point you should not be concerned with color, size, shape, or aesthetics. At first your concern should be only about process, not product. Concentrate on successfully completing the five steps necessary to make a bead:

1. Successfully heating the glass rod (no popping);

2. Adhering the hot glass to the mandrel (both must be sufficiently hot);

3. Winding the hot glass around the mandrel;

4. Successfully winding off (don't try to wind more hot glass than you have); and

5. Getting the finished bead into the blanket or vermiculite at the proper temperature.

Once these steps become second nature to you, you'll be able to think about the extra steps that go into making bigger, more elaborate beads.

Top left: Karen Ovington, acid-etched beads, 3.5 cm long (typical)
Photograph: Tom Van Eynde

Top right: Char Eagleton, *Swamp Ophelia*, sculptural accent beads, 3 x 3.8 cm (frog pendant)
Photograph: Evan Bracken

Bottom: Char Eagleton, mermaid torso, acid-etched, 3.1 cm high
Photograph: Evan Bracken

Jana Burnham, 1-to-5-strand necklace, basic beads and simple variations

Photograph: Wayne Torborg

EXTINGUISHING THE TORCH

When you're done working with the single-fuel torch, turn it off firmly to the right. If you see a small flame or glow at the base of the torch head, you have not turned it off completely. When you're done for the day, remove the torch head from the tank so that any gas remaining in the tank won't leak out. Remember that the torch head itself is still very hot, so be careful when removing it. Either use heat-resistant gloves or wait until it has cooled.

Extinguish an oxygen-propane torch by turning off the oxygen first, then the propane. Remember the *"POOP"* rule. I'm not sure who came up with this acronym, but it's been around forever. I first heard it from Bandhu Scott Dunham.

Turning ON		Shutting OFF	
P	O	O	P
Propane	Oxygen	Oxygen	Propane

When you're through working for the day, reverse the procedures you used for setting up. Shut off the torch valves, then the regulator valves, and then the tank valves. Now reopen the torch valves and bleed any residual gas from the lines. Finally, shut off the torch valves for good.

REMOVING YOUR BEAD FROM THE MANDREL

When your bead is cool, you can remove it from the mandrel by first soaking it in a cup of water for a minute or so to soften the separator and loosen the bead. (This also helps keep down the amount of dust in your studio.)

Above: Donna Sauers, pin with basic beads, 2 cm long (largest); bracelet with acid-etched beads, 9 mm long (typical)

Photograph: Evan Bracken

Right: Jana Burnham, *Trapeze Necklace*, dots and eyes, 6.4 x 1.3 cm (long bead)

Photographer: Ralph Gabriner

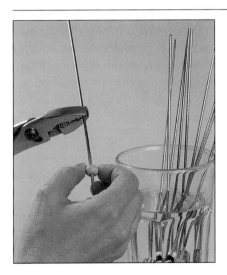

If you are unable to twist off the bead easily at this point, use a pair of pliers (I like vise-grip pliers for this) to grab your mandrel down below the bead. Then twist off the bead with your other hand. The pliers serve as a handle and give you extra leverage, which makes it easier to twist off the bead. You may also try grasping the bead

with a rubber jar lid opener while still holding the mandrel with a pair of pliers in your other hand. If the bead separator is still intact and won't release, try crunching it at both ends of the bead to help loosen the separator inside the bead. Then, if the bead is still stuck, try soaking it in the water for a

HOT TIP

AS A LAST RESORT, IF YOUR BEAD IS REALLY STUCK ONTO THE MANDREL YOU CAN TRY PUTTING IT IN A FREEZER OR PLACING JUST THE MANDREL IN ICE WATER FOR ABOUT 15 MINUTES. SOMETIMES THIS CONTRACTS THE STEEL ROD JUST ENOUGH TO ALLOW YOU TO SLIP OFF THE BEAD.

longer period of time; sometimes soaking it overnight can help loosen a stubborn bead.

Note: If the separator was disturbed under the bead as you were making it, and the hot glass actually came in contact with the steel rod, you may hear an ominous clicking as you try to twist the bead free. With a transparent bead, you can sometimes see where the separator is missing from a section of the mandrel under the bead. Ultimately, if your bead can't be removed from the mandrel, just chalk it up to experience and use the whole thing as a plant decoration.

You will be more prone to this problem if you work your glass too cold or if you overheat your mandrel. Applying too thick or too thin a coating of separator can also contribute to this problem. To save the mandrel for future use, cut it off just below the bead and use the shorter rod to make more beads.

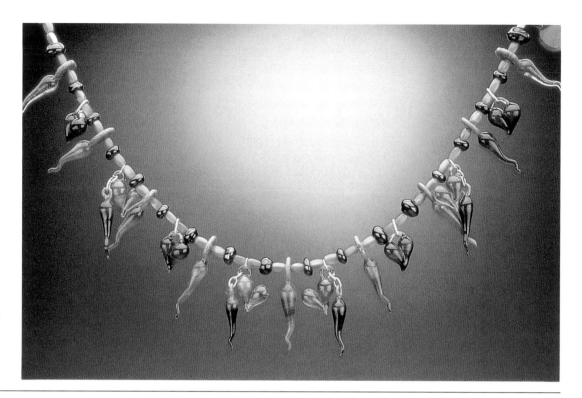

Ellie Burke, *Heartburn Necklace*, sculptural beads, 3.2 x 1 cm (peppers)

Photograph: William F. Lemke

FINISHING TOUCHES

A pipe cleaner and water should be sufficient to clean out the residue of bead separator from the holes in most of your beads.

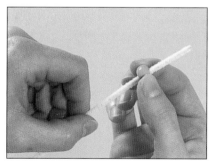

Real pipe cleaners designed for cleaning out tobacco pipes are better than the pipe cleaners designed for crafts; the real ones have metal and fiber mixed together for better abrasive action. If you find that pipe cleaners won't work, special metal bead core scrapers are also available. They're much faster, sturdier, and easier to use than pipe cleaners and are the best way

I've found to clean out the hole in the bead. If your bead is transparent and you think any remaining bead separator is distracting, try soaking your bead in an undiluted liquid toilet bowl cleaner or a lime scale remover for half an hour, or even as long as overnight for severe cases. Be careful, though; this stuff is potent!

Remember—the longer and harder you work your bead during the forming process, the more firmly the bead separator will adhere to the center of the bead. Don't let this be discouraging; if you look closely, you'll notice that most of the wound beads you buy have a bit of bead separator in their holes.

To remove burrs, a fine diamond file will do a good job of smoothing any rough or sharp spots around the hole of the bead. The best tool for this, however, is an engraving pen or motorized mini-tool that has a rotating action with a small diamond bit. Removing burrs is important; a sharp edge may make the bead uncomfortable to wear

and can even cut through the stringing material of a necklace or bracelet.

Many surface flaws, such as remnants of bead separator or fiber blanket, vermiculite marks, and even grayish color reduction, can be removed by using an acid etching solution for glass. This solution actually removes the surface layer of the glass bead. You can selectively etch your bead by covering parts of it with glue or nail polish so that only the exposed part gets etched. Acid etching produces a matte satin finish on your bead, which looks particularly nice if you leave some parts of the bead, such as dots or millefiori, shiny.

Diamond grinding tools such as a motorized mini-tool or an engraving pen are another way of altering the surface of your bead and adding interest.

The moral is: don't despair! Even if your best bead has bead separator or a dirty spot on the surface, let it inspire you to create a new surface design!

SIMPLE VARIATIONS

Kelly Niemann, dots, trails, and squiggle lines, 1.6 cm long (longest)

Photograph: Evan Bracken

Top: Audrie Wiesenfelder, *Amethyst/Blue Tassel Necklace*, grooved beads, 1.9 cm long (largest)

Photograph: Tom Van Eynde

Bottom: Heather Trimlett, cone, 1.9 x 2.5 cm

Photograph: Evan Bracken

SHAPING YOUR BEADS

USING GRAVITY

Once you feel comfortable making a simple wound bead, you've mastered the hardest part. Now the fun begins.

By now you've learned how important it is to keep your mandrel turning when the glass is hot. Hot glass is a lot like thick honey, and it will flow downhill if given a chance.

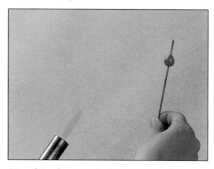

Use this characteristic to your advan-

tage to shape your beads; for a teardrop-shaped bead, experiment with holding the mandrel either uphill or downhill. You can do this at any point in the melting process. If you allow it to drip farther than you want, just reheat and slant the mandrel back the other way.

This is a useful technique; it can be used to even out a lumpy bead or to recess the hole farther into a bead.

USING A MARVER

To continue shaping and texturing your bead, you will need some type of marver. A marver is a smooth, heat-proof surface that is generally made of graphite or metal, such as aluminum or steel. Any clean, smooth metal or stone that won't melt or crack when it comes in contact with hot glass will work.

You can use this to roll and press your bead in order to get different shapes and add interest and variety to your beads.

One important fact to keep in mind whenever touching your hot glass to a cold tool, such as a marver, is that you have just chilled a small area on the surface of your bead.

This introduces stress into your bead;

the glass that contacts the marver actually freezes, becomes stiff, and produces a whorl on the surface of the bead that resembles a fingerprint. The rest of the bead is still fluid, and the difference can cause your bead to break. For this reason, it's very important to "flash" the bead back into the flame immediately after using any shaping tools, and it's best to even out the heat throughout the bead after shaping. Of course, you don't want to overdo it and lose any interesting details or textures that you have just added; you need to reheat it only enough to remove the chill marks. It will take some practice to develop a sense of how much reheating is necessary.

PRESSED BEADS

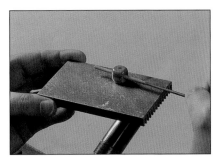

You can press your bead against the marver on two sides to form a disk or tabular bead (a flattened bead of any shape), three sides for a triangular bead, four sides for a cube, etc.

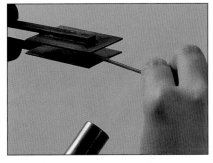

A quick and easy way to make a disk-shaped bead is to use flatteners—simply hold the molten bead between the two plates and squeeze. Don't flatten your bead too much; the wall

Top: James Smircich, gravity-formed lines (left), 4.8 cm long; gravity-formed design from stacked dots (right), 3.3 cm long

Photograph: Evan Bracken

Bottom: Inara Knight, tabular-shaped pressed bead, 4 x 3.2 cm

Photograph: Evan Bracken

thickness should be at least as great as the diameter of your mandrel. After each contact with the marver or flatteners, remember to reheat your bead. Experiment!

CYLINDER BEADS

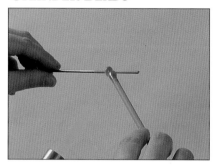

For a cylinder, start by making a basic bead as you normally would; then continue to heat the glass rod. Wind another basic bead alongside the first one.

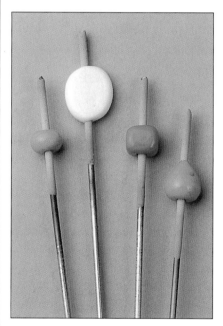

Cindy Jenkins, basic bead, .7 x 1.1 cm; flattened disk, 2 x 1.8 cm; cube, 1 x 1.2 cm; gravity-formed bead, 1.5 x 1.3 cm

Photograph: Evan Bracken

Jana Burnham, various shapes, 5.1 x 5.1 cm (largest)

Photograph: Wayne Torborg

40

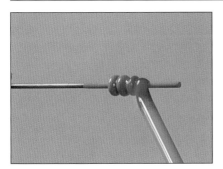

Repeat once or twice, until your cylinder is as long as you want it.

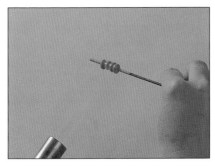

Then heat the entire bead in the flame until it has an even glow.

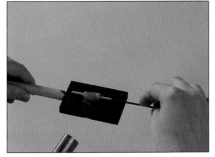

To even out the scalloped surface of the cylinder, gently roll your bead against a

smooth, hard surface, such as a marver or graphite paddle. Press very lightly when you first come in contact with the marver so that you don't inadvertently flatten one side of the bead, making it difficult to roll. It's best to have the mandrel actually rolling in your hand before the bead itself comes in direct contact with the marver. If you roll it back and forth, it's easy to create flat spots where you change the direction of your roll. To avoid this, be careful not to pause at the end of the roll with the bead still on the marver. Either change directions instantly, without hesitation, or lift the bead off the marver between rolls. A torch marver works well for this because you can support the bead on the shelf and roll evenly.

BICONES

For a bicone-shaped bead, begin by making a cylinder.

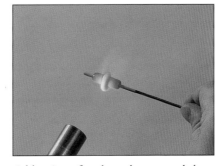

Add a ring of molten glass around the center; then heat the entire bead until

the central ring partially melts into it.

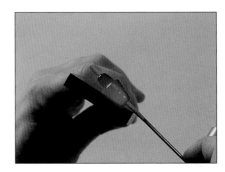

Tip the mandrel so that you're touching just the bottom third of your bead to the marver and roll in this angled position until the end of the bead forms a cone.

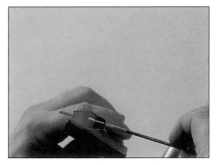

Now heat the other end of the bead and tip the mandrel in the opposite direction to shape the top third.

Kate Fowle, black-and-gold frit bead necklace with clear overwraps on accent beads, 2.3 cm long (typical larger bead)

Photograph: Evan Bracken

GROOVED BEADS

By rolling your bead on a grooved marver, you can create a ridged texture on its surface. This is a great way to disguise the fact that your original wound bead may not have been perfectly even and round. Adding grooves to the hot bead provides extra dimension and sparkle.

You can roll the bead vertically, horizontally, or diagonally for different looks.

For another effect, roll your bead twice on a grooved marver, the second time at a different angle from the first. This can create a crosshatching "pineapple" appearance. Try selectively marvering just the ends of your beads for yet another look.

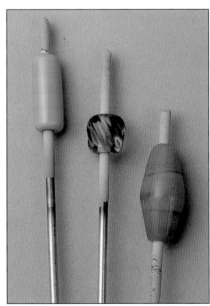

Cindy Jenkins, cylinder, 2 cm long; grooved bead, 1 cm long; bicone, 2.6 cm long

Photograph: Evan Bracken

OVERWRAPS

As you've already seen, there are many variations you can make just with "basic" beads. Now we'll add more volume of glass—either to make larger beads or to mix different colored rods together. This approach involves *overwrapping* a basic bead by winding more hot glass around it. The second layer of hot glass can be more of the same glass used in the basic bead, or you can introduce another color.

To start, make a basic bead and let it cool a bit so that it's stiff. Periodically flash the bead by putting it back into the flame so that it doesn't crack from overcooling, but avoid reheating it to a molten state. You'll want this initial "core" bead to be fairly stiff so that you can use it as a foundation for additional work.

While still holding your mandrel with the core bead in one hand, start heating another glass rod with your other hand.

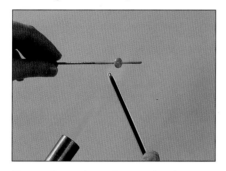

Remember to keep the core bead warm by periodically flashing it in the flame. You don't want the bead to be fluid; if it's somewhat molten, you won't be able to control the overwrap because the core bead will move together with the new rod as you wrap it.

Overwrapping is very similar to making a basic bead—the initial basic bead functions much as the mandrel does, and you're essentially winding another basic bead on top of the first one.

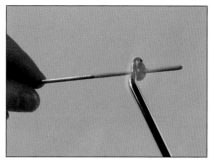

Touch the tip of your hot glass rod to the middle of your core bead and start rotating the mandrel until you've gone all the way around.

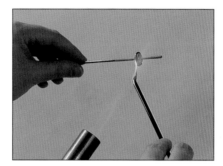

Now wind off. With a little practice, you'll be able to heat the correct amount of glass to get all the way around the bead. If you don't make it all the way around on your first pass, wind off and heat more glass. Start where you left off and add more glass until you have an even amount all the way around.

Once you've applied your overwrap, you can either leave the overwrap standing out so that your bead looks like Saturn, you can try marvering just the overwrap itself, or you can continue heating the bead until the overwrap is completely absorbed and the bead surface is smooth again.

Beads with a transparent color core and a filigrana overwrap are especially beautiful!

Top: Audrie Wiesenfelder, grooved tabular bead, 3.5 x 2.5 cm

Photograph: Evan Bracken

Bottom: Jana Burnham, clear overwrap, 1 x 1.5 cm

Photograph: Evan Bracken

MULTICOLORED BEADS

For a bicolored bead, start the same way as you did for an overwrap: make a basic bead, let it stiffen up, and periodically flash it in the flame so that it doesn't crack. Now heat up another glass rod.

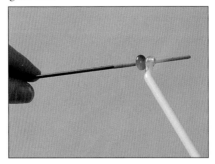

This time, instead of wrapping the new color on top of the core bead, wrap the second color right next to it. Heat the whole bead evenly and lightly marver it to seal the seam between the two segments.

In order to avoid trapping an air bubble between the two halves of your bead, you can do one of two things. The first approach is to make sure your glass rod is really molten before adding it onto the stiff core bead and, rather than simply wrapping the hot glass around the mandrel, use a push/pull movement to squeeze out any air pockets that might create bubbles.

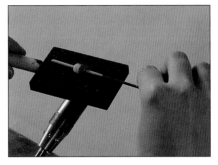

If that doesn't work for you, try leaving a narrow gap between the two beads; then heat and marver them together.

Now try a triple-wrapped bead. Again start by wrapping a basic bead, letting it cool, and periodically flashing it in and out of the flame.

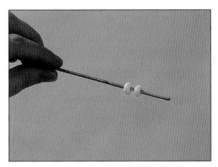

This time, however, continue to heat the same glass rod you just used for the basic bead, and wrap another basic bead with a ¼-inch (6 mm) gap between the two. After letting the second bead set up a bit, continue to flash both beads periodically without letting them get too fluid again.

Top: Tom Holland, black-and-white core with amber overwrap, 1 x 1.5 cm

Photograph: Evan Bracken

Bottom: Jana Burnham, earrings, clear overwrap, 5.1 cm long

Photograph: Ralph Gabriner

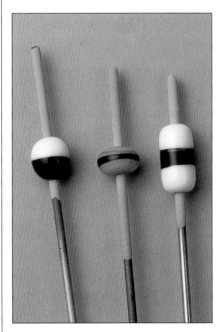

Cindy Jenkins, bicolor (left), 1 x 1.2 cm; overwrap (center), .7 x 1.2 cm; triple-wrapped bead (right), 1.9 cm long

Photograph: Evan Bracken

Right: Gina Lambert, black-and-white bicolored beads, 1.8 x 1.5 cm (typical)

Photograph: Evan Bracken

Far right: Kimberley Adams, multicolored dangles, 2.2 x 1.3 cm (rectangular bead)

Photograph: Evan Bracken

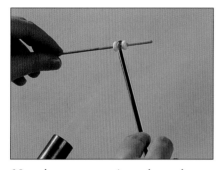

Next, heat a contrasting color and wrap it into the gap between the first two beads. Lightly marver and reheat the whole triple-wrapped bead.

For more variety, try the same approach with three different colors. Apply a filigrana overwrap on top of the middle color or try an overwrap on all three colors. Experiment to see the result of using the same color of fil-igrana for all three overwraps and com-pare it to the effect of using three different colors. As a final step, try applying spiral grooves to the surface with your dual-action marver.

SPOTS, DOTS & EYES

To get a random pattern of color spots on your bead, you can use *frit*, which is simply crushed glass in varying sizes. To make small amounts of frit, make sure your slip-joint pliers are clean and use them to crush some of your left-over ends of glass rods into a catch container. Be sure to wear eye protec-tion! The small glass chips that result are called frit. (If you don't want to make your own, frit is available pre-made and sifted for size.)

Sprinkle some frit on the smooth sur-face of your marver and roll your hot bead in it. The frit will adhere to the bead's hot surface. For a uniquely tex-tured surface, heat the frit on the bead until the frit is well stuck but remains chunky. If you prefer a smooth bead, continue to heat the frit on the bead until it melts completely into the sur-face. Either smooth or textured, the frit will add a random pattern of color spots to your bead.

For more controlled dots, use a con-trasting color rod. Make a basic bead, let it cool a bit, and hold it just behind the flame.

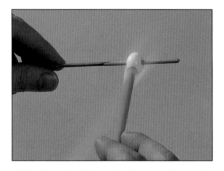

After heating the end of your glass rod until just the tip is glowing, touch the molten tip to the core bead.

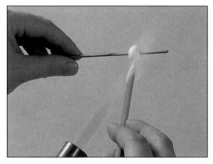

Quickly stretch the rod back about an inch (2.5 cm) while turning the dot *toward* (thumb moving down), not *away from*, the flame. If you wait a few seconds, the heat of the flame will cut through the stretched portion of the glass and leave a dot of color on the surface of the bead.

HOT **TIP**

HERE ARE A FEW METHODS FOR MAKING LARGER QUANTITIES OF FRIT. (REMEMBER THOSE SAFETY GLASSES!)

- DOUBLE-BAG YOUR GLASS BITS, PUT THEM IN A CARDBOARD BOX, AND SMASH THEM WITH A HAMMER.

- MAKE OR BUY A "GLASS CRUSHER." THIS IS ESSENTIALLY A STEEL PIPE, SEALED AT THE BOTTOM, WITH A CLOSE-FITTING PESTLE.

- IF YOU HAVE A KILN, YOU CAN PUT YOUR SCRAPS IN A HEAT-PROOF CONTAINER INSIDE THE KILN AND INCREASE THE HEAT TO APPROXIMATELY 1000°F (540°C). REMOVE THE CONTAINER, WEARING HEAT-PROOF GLOVES, AND DUMP THE HOT GLASS INTO A CLEAN METAL BUCKET FILLED WITH COLD WATER. THE COLD WATER WILL CRACKLE THE HOT PIECES OF GLASS, AND THEY WILL EASILY BREAK APART. THIS TRADITIONAL TECHNIQUE EXPLAINS OUR USE OF THE WORD *FRIT*—IT COMES FROM AN ITALIAN WORD MEANING "FRY."

- IF YOU WANT TO GET REALLY NUTTY (AND NOISY!) AND MAKE *LOTS* OF FRIT, YOU CAN USE AN OLD GARBAGE DISPOSER MOUNTED INSIDE A METAL BAR-REL. JUST FEED YOUR LEFTOVER SCRAPS OF GLASS INTO THE GARBAGE DIS-POSAL; THEN SIFT THE REMAINS FOR VARIOUS SIZES OF GLASS BITS. (YOU MAY HAVE TO SIFT OR USE A MAGNET TO REMOVE ANY METAL FLAKES THAT THE DISPOSER INADVERTENTLY DEPOSITS INTO THE MIX.)

Opposite left: Tom Holland, *Golden Zhou*, dots and eyes, 3.2 x 2 cm

Photographer: Tom Holland

Opposite right: Susan Simonds, *Happy Bead* (left), 1.4 x 2 cm; *Jungle Bead* (center), 2 x 2.4 cm; *Jungle Bead* (right), 3.8 cm long; all dots on dots

Photograph: Evan Bracken

Right: Ellie Burke, *Blue Corn* (left), 3.2 cm; *Peruvian Corn* (center), 1.9 cm; *Blue on Blue Corn* (right), 3.5 cm long; all dotted beads

Photograph: William F. Lemke

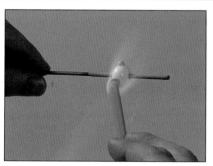

Briefly heat this dot before taking the bead out of the flame. Repeat this process, adding dots to as many areas as you like. As with all glass "additions," you have the choice of heating the dots until they absorb into the bead and become flush with the surface or heating them less and having the dots stand out in partial relief.

To make an *eye bead*, simply add another dot of contrasting color right

on top of the first dot. You can get as crazy as you want, adding multiple dots on top of dots, but if you leave them protruding very far, remember to heat all the dots sufficiently so that they adhere firmly to the core bead. If you don't, the dots may pop apart later. Also be aware that if the dot stacks are too tall they can be fragile as well as uncomfortable for the wearer.

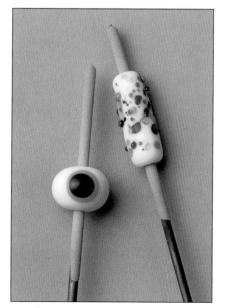

Cindy Jenkins, eye bead, 1.1 x 1.5 cm; frit, 2.5 cm long

Photograph: Evan Bracken

STRIPES AND TRAILS

Adding stripes and trails takes a little more practice than adding simple dots does. The trick here is to focus your flame on the glass rod and keep the bead underneath the flame as you trail the hot glass onto it. Holding just the rod in the flame creates a reservoir of hot glass to trail over the relatively cool bead. If the bead is hot and the glass rod is cold, you can actually remove glass from the bead instead of adding it.

For stripes, make a basic bead and marver it into a cylindrical shape. This gives you a more consistent shape to trail onto and makes it easier to learn this technique. Hold the bead just under the flame while heating the top ⅜ inch (1 cm) of a contrasting glass rod.

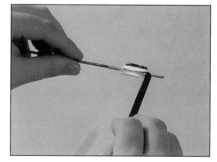

Touch the hot tip of your glass rod to one end of your bead, stretch back a

bit, and draw a line across the length of the bead. Touch down at the opposite end, pull back, and melt or snap the end of the hot glass off the bead.

Now let's add a spiral trail to your bead. Again, it's easier to learn to trail onto the relatively flat surface of a cylindrical bead than onto the rounded face of a spherical one. Make another basic bead and marver it into a cylindrical shape. Holding the warm bead just under the flame, heat the top ⅜ inch (1 cm) of your glass rod.

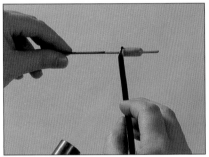

Touch the hot glass to one side of the bead, using just enough pressure to make it stick but not so much that it leaves a blob of glass at the start of your trail. Stretch the glass just as if you were going to make a dot, but this time rotate your mandrel away from the flame. This allows the stretched glass to trail over your bead and prevents it from being melted through by the flame as it would for a dot.

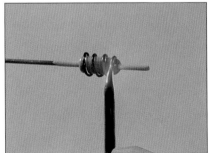

Continue rolling until you have a glass thread trailed around the entire bead.

Kimberley Adams, *Autumn Necklace*, spiral trails and dots, 3.8 x 3.2 cm (focal bead)

Photograph: Jerry Anthony

Above: Barbara Thomas-Yerace, squiggle line, 1.2 x 2 cm

Photograph: Evan Bracken

Top right: Jacob Fishman, queen bee, 1.7 x 2.7 cm; Sue Richers Elgar, drones, all with spiral trails, 1.6 x 1.1 cm (typical)

Photograph: Evan Bracken

Right: Barbara Thomas-Yerace, *Snakes*, spiral beads, 3.5 cm long (largest)

Photograph: Evan Bracken

Practice this process until you can trail completely around the bead several times, from one end to the other. Try trailing a spiral in the opposite direction, using a contrasting color, or try mixing spirals, spots, and stripes. Keep practicing until you can get a nice smooth trail on your beads.

If you use filigrana rod in place of an opaque color, the spiral trail will look

TOM HOLLAND HAS A SIMPLE BUT EFFECTIVE METHOD FOR REMOVING THE SMALL BUMP THAT OCCURS AT THE START OF YOUR WOUND SPIRAL: AFTER COMPLETING A SPIRAL TRAIL, ROLL YOUR BEAD ON THE MARVER IN THE *OPPOSITE* DIRECTION OF THE WIND.

thinner and more clearly defined. This is because your eye dismisses the clear casing and sees only the color core. The clear glass also keeps your trail lines from bleeding into each other, no matter how close together you make your trails.

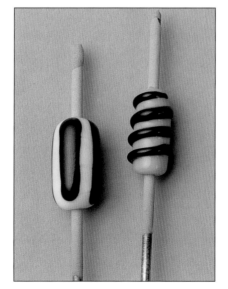

Cindy Jenkins, stripes, 2.2 cm long; spiral trail, 2.1 cm long

Photograph: Evan Bracken

PULLING STRINGER

In addition to using full-size glass rods to decorate the surface of your beads, you may want to have glass stringer. Stringer, or glass spaghetti cane, is a very thin rod of glass—often only about 1/16 inch (1.5 mm) thick. Stringer is useful for adding fine detail to your core beads. Many stained glass stores carry stringer in a wide palette of colors made by Bullseye glass. If you're using tested-compatible Bullseye or Uroboros for your bead, this will work fine, but if you're using Effetre glass, you'll need to make your own; stringer made by Bullseye is not compatible with Effetre glass.

There are several techniques for pulling stringer; experiment with each one to decide your favorite.

SINGLE-ROD METHOD

Start heating your glass rod in the center, instead of at the end.

Heather Trimlett, *Teapots*, stringer, 3.8 cm high (typical)

Photograph: Patty Hulet

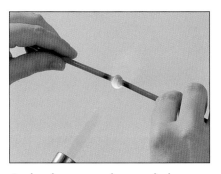

As the glass gets molten, push the two ends toward the middle to create a hot ball of glass.

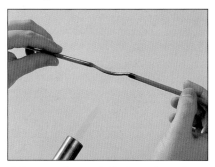

When you have a ball about ½ inch (1.3 cm) in diameter, come out of the flame and pull both ends of the rod to create a long stringer in the center. Melt or break the finished stringer from the parent rods. Practice making stringer this way a few times, pulling both slowly and quickly to become familiar with how the glass moves. If necessary, holding the rods vertically may help even out your pull. Place the thicker end on top so that gravity helps the glass start stretching.

Because stringer is so thin, it can be allowed to air-cool and doesn't need to be placed in the fiber blanket.

DUAL-ROD TECHNIQUE

This approach, which I learned from Tom Holland, is very similar to the previous one.

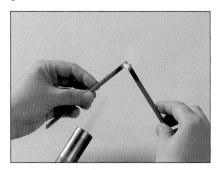

Start with two pieces of rod and hold them in an inverted V formation, with the flame at the bottom of the intersection. As the two rods heat and stick together, push them toward each other to form a molten ball.

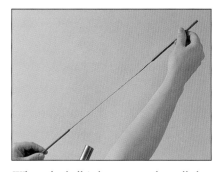

When the ball is large enough, pull the molten glass out into a stringer as you did with the single-rod method.

PLIERS METHOD

Heat the end of your glass rod just as if you were going to make a bead.

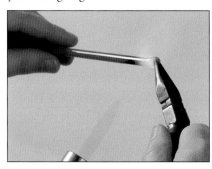

When the end of the rod is hot, grab the glowing glass with needle-nose pliers and slowly start to pull. Because I'm right-handed, I prefer to have the glass in my left hand and the pliers in my right; you may want to reverse this.

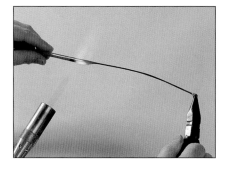

It's important to remember to keep the thick part of your glass rod in the flame, not the thin portion that you just pulled. If you continue to heat the thin section, it will quickly melt through, and you'll end up with a very short stringer. Keep the flame *behind* the area you are actually pulling and don't rotate the rod as you pull.

The thickness of the stringer will be determined both by how hot the glass is and by how quickly or slowly you pull. The quicker the pull, the thinner the stringer. Remember, your stringer doesn't necessarily need to be perfectly consistent in diameter throughout its length.

EMERGENCY STRINGER

Oops! You're in the middle of a bead and discover that you don't have any of the right color stringer on hand. You'll have to improvise. While keeping your bead warm so that it doesn't break, heat up the color rod you need, letting it ball up on the end.

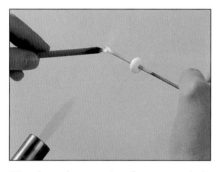

Now heat the very tip of your mandrel and press the ball of glass onto it.

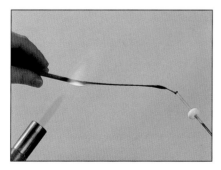

Holding the glass rod in the flame, pull the mandrel away until you have enough glass stringer. The stringer will chill quickly, and you can break it off

the mandrel by wiggling the stringer back and forth. You may need to reshape the tip with the flame before you can use it. Tom Holland calls this "911" stringer.

If you're planning to make decorated beads, pull stringer in several different colors before you start making the beads themselves. You'll want to have a variety available for decorating techniques when you need them. When working with various colors, you'll find that some are softer and more fluid when heated, making them more difficult to use for pulling stringer. Just keep practicing.

HOT TIP

IF IT SEEMS AS THOUGH YOU NEED THREE HANDS WHEN YOU WANT TO SHAPE THE END OF A PIECE OF STRINGER, IT'S ALL RIGHT TO SET DOWN YOUR BEAD FOR A FEW SECONDS. AFTER WARMING THE BEAD TO A GLOW IN THE FLAME, EITHER SET THE MANDREL UPRIGHT IN YOUR MANDREL BLOCK OR LAY IT OVER YOUR ROD REST. THE HOT BEAD SHOULD BE IN CONTACT ONLY WITH AIR, NOT A HARD SURFACE THAT COULD CHILL IT ON ONE SIDE. LAYING THE BEAD ON A FIBER BLANKET FOR A FEW SECONDS IS ALSO ACCEPTABLE. WHENEVER YOU SET YOUR BEAD ASIDE FOR A FEW MOMENTS, MAKE SURE THAT IT'S NOT SO HOT THAT GRAVITY WILL CHANGE ITS SHAPE.

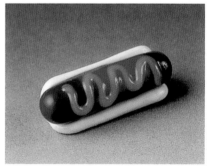

Top: Kimberley Osibin, *Danäe*, stringer-decorated beads and pendant
Photograph: George Post

Center: Al Janelle, hot dog with mustard, 2.5 cm
Photograph: Evan Bracken

Bottom: Jana Burnham, cones, 3.5 cm long (largest)
Photograph: Evan Bracken

Left: Kelly Niemann, black-and-white bracelet, stringer and dots, 8 mm (typical)
Photograph: Evan Bracken

Above: Inara Knight, tube beads with stringer and frit, 6 cm long (typical)
Photograph: Evan Bracken

STRIPED STRINGER

I learned this trick from Tom Holland, and he swears that it's worth at least ten bucks!

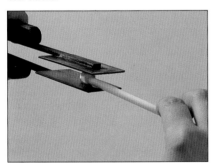

Heat the end of your glass rod until it forms a uniformly glowing ball; then squash the hot glass to form a disk. This can be done by using bead flatteners or by squeezing the bead between your graphite paddle and marver.

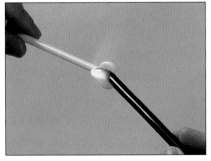

Using a contrasting color, apply a stripe horizontally across the center of one side of the disk.

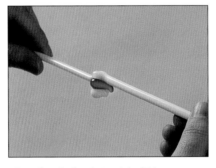

Now, here's the $10 trick: Take your original color and add it along both sides of the contrasting stripe. This will create a support dam and keep the contrasting color from spreading out as you get it hot enough to pull.

Pull as you would an ordinary stringer, but be careful not to twist it so that the stripe stays all on one side.

When applying striped stringer to your bead, make sure that the stripe stays on top and doesn't roll over and get hidden. Those who see your trailed bead with its tiny contrasting stripe on top of a stripe will be very impressed with your mastery of stringer applications.

Cindy Jenkins, assorted stringer
Photograph: Evan Bracken

FUN WITH STRINGER

Okay, by now you should have some stringer pulled in different colors—maybe you even tried making some striped stringer. Let's have some fun!

You can use your stringer to apply dots and spiral trails, just as you did with your regular glass rods. Stringer will give a smaller, tighter pattern to your bead, which is essential for more complex designs. Initially stringer will be more difficult to work with because it reacts to the heat of the flame so quickly. You may want to work a little higher in the flame or turn the flame down slightly to gain control. The technique is exactly the same as with regular glass rod, but it goes much more quickly and leaves finer detail.

FREEFORM DESIGNS

If at first you find it frustrating to trail your stringer onto a bead, try freeform drawing instead.

Just make squiggly lines and trails in different colors until you feel more in

control. In a random pattern, anything goes, so you'll still end up with a great-looking bead. Once you can apply a fairly straight band or stripe to your bead, there are lots of ways to manipulate the lines to create different patterns.

TWISTED BANDS

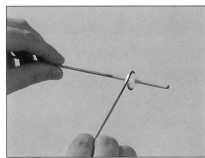

After making a basic bead of any shape, wrap a contrasting color of stringer around it to form a thin band. Heat one spot on the band until it is glowing, come out of the flame, and use a cold piece of stringer to twist the band.

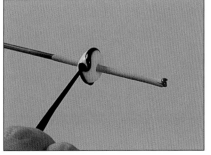

The twisting stringer should be fairly thick and have a hard, flat end. Plant the end firmly on the glowing band

Top left: James Smircich, *Pinwheel Medallion*, twisted line, 4.2 x 3.3 cm

Photograph: Evan Bracken

Top center: Tom Holland (left), black bicone with twisted dots, 3.3 cm high; Susan Simonds (right), *Spring*, twisted dots, 1.7 x 2 cm

Photograph: Evan Bracken

Top right: Michael Barley, spiral trail twisted with a star millefiore, 4.2 cm high

Photograph: Evan Bracken

Bottom: Brian Kerkvliet, twisted dots, 2.7 cm high

Photograph: Evan Bracken

Far left: Isis Pearl Ray (top), undersea bead with octopus, 3 cm long; Audrie Wiesenfelder (lower left), blue cylinder, 4 cm long; Peggy Prielozny (center), three bicones, 2.7 x 1.5 cm; Audrie Wiesenfelder (far right), green tabular bead, 4 x 2 cm; all decorated with stringer

Photograph: Evan Bracken

Left: Kristina Logan, blue floral bead, twisted dots, 3.2 x 1.9 cm

Photograph: Dean Powel

and twist. After completing the twist, wiggle the stringer back and forth until it breaks free. If it seems stubborn, blow on the stringer and wiggle again, but don't try to force it. After a few seconds, the thin stringer will cool enough to snap free. Now move on to an adjacent area, heat, and twist. Continue around the bead until you've finished the pattern.

If you use a contrasting color stringer to do the twisting, each twist will have a contrasting dot in the middle because as you snap the stringer away, a small dot of glass from the twisting stringer is left behind.

Twisted Multicolored Bead

You can produce a similar result by twisting the joint between any two colors on a multicolored bead. Using a bicolored bead as an example, construct your bead as usual and, while the glass is still hot, place your stringer onto the line where the two colors join.

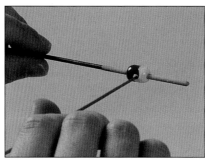

Twist the stringer to make a small spiral at the joint.

Twisted Dots

This twisting technique also works with groups of dots. If you put your dots around a central point, you can place your stringer into that central point and twist.

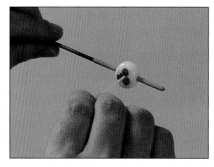

This pulls the dots around into a whirlpool design. By using a contrasting center dot, you can create a flowerlike motif.

Twisted Stripes

To create a twisted stripe effect, lay a short stripe across your bead.

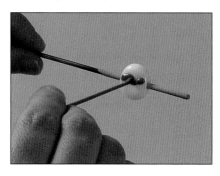

Touch your stringer to the center of the stripe and twist.

Pinched Chains

Stringer also can be used to create a chain pattern.

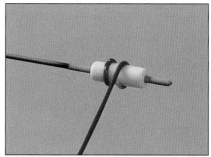

Place two parallel bands of stringer around the equator of your bead, leaving a narrow space between them.

Jana Burnham, gold leaf with transparent stringer

Photograph: Ralph Gabriner

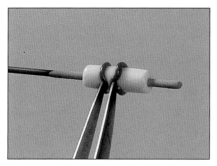

Heat one side; then use sharp, pointed tweezers to pinch the bands together.

For greater variety, use a contrasting color stringer to place dots at all the pinched junctions or try using different colors for the bands, making a multi-colored chain. Another alternative is to make a chain with three or four bands of stringer trails.

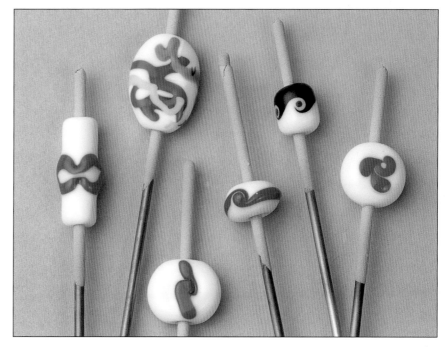

Cindy Jenkins, left to right: pinched chain, 2.6 cm long; freeform stringer, 2.4 x 1.8 cm; twisted stripe, 1.5 x 1.8 cm; twisted band, .8 x 1.5 cm; twisted bicolor, 1.6 cm long; twisted dots, 1.5 x 1.6 cm

Photograph: Evan Bracken

RAKED PATTERNS

Once you've added dots, stripes, or a trail to your bead, you can manipulate these simple designs with a bead rake. This is a metal tool, preferably stainless steel or tungsten, that has a straight or hooked point at the end (some tools have both, one at each end). You can use this tool to drag and manipulate hot glass on the surface of a bead. As long as the rake is kept cool, it will not stick to the glass. Keep a cup of cold water handy and dip the hot end of the rake in the water to chill it after each use.

DOTS AND STRIPES

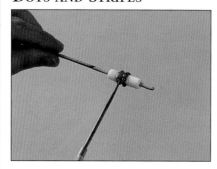

Try raking dots by making a single or double row of dots around the equator of your bead, then raking down through the center of the row to produce a leafy or heart-shaped effect.

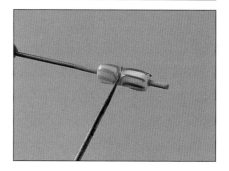

For a raked stripe pattern, lay parallel horizontal stripes along the length of the bead and rake.

Now try the same process with your striped stringer to multiply the design possibilities!

RAKED LOOPS

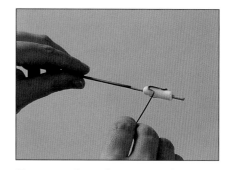

To create a looped pattern, make a cylindrical bead and decorate it with stringer trailed in a wide squiggle around the bead.

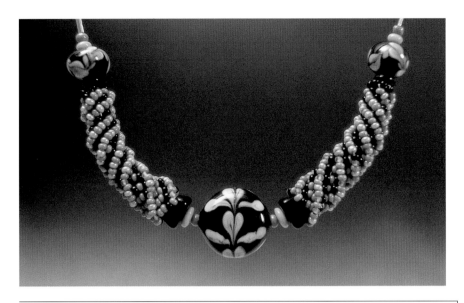

Now rake down the center to pull the squiggle into loops.

As with the twisting techniques, if you substitute a contrasting colored stringer for the bead rake to do your raking, you will leave a fine line of the contrasting color on your bead.

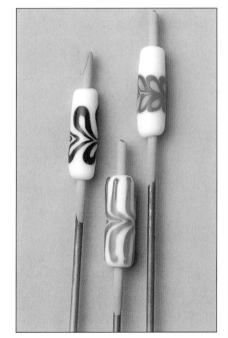

HOT TIP

Cindy Jenkins, raked loop (left), 2.7 cm long; raked stripes (center), 2.7 cm long; raked dots (right), 2.7 cm long

Photograph: Evan Bracken

Top left: Bernadette Mahfood, *Helix Bracelet*, raked dots, 1.3 x 1.9 cm (center bead)

Photograph: Bernadette Mahfood

Top right: Bernadette Mahfood, *Morning Glory Beads*, raked dots, 1.3 x 1.9 cm

Photograph: Bernadette Mahfood

Bottom: Susan Simonds, *Pastel Vine* (left), 2.8 x 2.6 cm; *Blue Vine* (right), 2.7 x 2.6 cm; both with raked dots

Photograph: Evan Bracken

TAKING THE NEXT STEP

Kate Fowle, *Hieroglyphic Necklace*, enamels, 3.5 cm (pendant)

Photograph: Evan Bracken

Kristen Frantzen Orr,
Green Botanical, blended
colors, 2.5 cm (focal bead)

Photograph: Jeff Scovil

MIXING COLORS

It may be hard to believe when you first start making beads that a palette of more than 100 colors would ever seem inadequate. Eventually, though, you'll need a particular shade, or you'll want to make some beads to match something very specific. You'll need to get creative and mix your own colors.

Start easy—with just two colors in equal amounts. Select two colors that you think will combine to create the new color you would like to have.

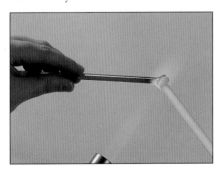

Heat the ends of both rods simultaneously and push them together in the flame. The fun part about this is that you can twist, turn, stir, and distort as much as you want—that's the idea!

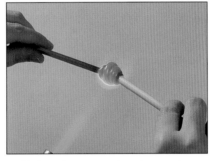

Roll the colors around and around each other until you get a homogenous mix (or maybe you'd rather have a more marbled appearance).

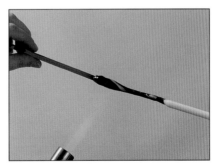

When you like the results, pull the central mass out into a rod of the desired thickness.

Try different combinations and keep a log of the colors and approximate proportions used. Mixing glass isn't like mixing paint: yellow and blue don't always equal green, and some colors look like mud when mixed together. (A little black mixed with white produces a deep violet, not the expected gray.) Occasionally you'll find a combination that simply won't mix together at all.

HOT TIP

I LIKE TO USE UP MY SCRAP GLASS WHEN MIXING COLORS. AFTER HEATING BOTH MIXING RODS, USE ONE HOT END TO PICK UP A SCRAP PIECE ABOUT ½ INCH (1.3 CM) LONG AND MIX IT RIGHT IN WITH THE OTHER ROD.

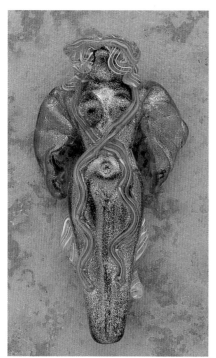

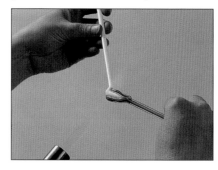

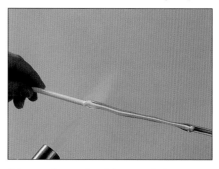

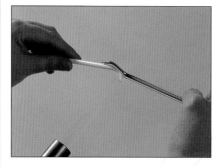

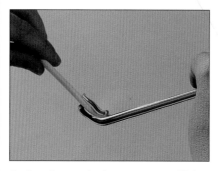

Ribbon Cane

Ribbon cane adds lots of detail to your beads with a minimal amount of effort. For your first attempt, a three-striped ribbon is a good choice. Select two colors, one for the center of the ribbon and a second that contrasts well with the first. Holding one rod in each hand, heat about 1 inch (2.5 cm) of both rods simultaneously.

When both ends are glowing, lay one color on top of the other as if you were applying toothpaste to a toothbrush; then melt the top color completely off the lower rod. While continuing to keep the double rod warm, heat up another inch (2.5 cm) of the contrasting colored rod. Apply a second stripe of the contrasting color along the bottom side of the center color, beginning at the point where the single rod becomes a double.

Rather than melt the new piece off the rod as you did the first time, heat the bottom rod and sharply bend it up to connect with the ends of the first two stripes. Then bend the bottom rod back down to the center so that both handles are centered with each other.

Next, heat the center color (now also functioning as the left handle) at the point where it is still a single rod.

Bend this rod down and then up so that it catches both of the contrasting stripes.

Heat and stretch without twisting to form a long, flat striped ribbon.

Once you've mastered the technique, try making a five-layer ribbon cane. Try slightly twisting the ribbon as you pull it. Play with it!

Ribbon cane can be added to your bead by either of two methods. You can apply the ribbon as if it were a simple glass rod, making a trail around the bead, or you can snip pieces off the ribbon and apply them on edge. (Brian Kerkvliet uses this technique as a quick and easy way to make the fins on his fish beads.)

Top: Jana Burnham, cylinder bead with ribbon cane, 4 cm long

Photograph: Evan Bracken

Bottom: Leah Fairbanks, *Amethyst Angel,* ribbon cane hair and decoration, 5.1 cm high

Photograph: George Post

TWISTIES

Twisties are simply a more advanced form of stringer. Using two or more rods of different colors, you can create stringer with delicate barber-pole patterns.

PLIERS METHOD

Select two contrasting colors of glass rod and tape them together with masking tape in two locations, starting about 6 inches (15 cm) back from the ends of the rods. Spend a little more time introducing this "double" rod into the flame, as you're heating twice as much mass as you have been. When the glass is heated, either pinch the ends together with pliers or press both sides down on the marver to squeeze the rods together. The glass should be in your dominant hand and the pliers in your other hand.

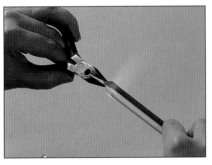

When the pinched end of the glass is glowing, grasp it with needle-nose pliers.

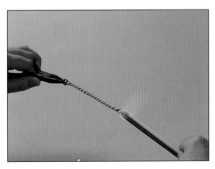

Start twisting the rods as you hold and pull slightly with the pliers. Following the same procedure as when making regular stringer, keep the thick (double) portion of the rods in the flame as you

twist and pull. This may feel awkward at first, but keep trying.

If you forget to keep shifting the twisted glass out of the flame, the heat will cause it to twist tighter and thinner until it melts through, resulting in very short twisties. Keep your eye on the flame and think to yourself, "twist-move, twist-move, twist-move," until it becomes second nature.

GLASS ROD TECHNIQUE

Another way to make twisties is to hold two contrasting rods, one in each hand, and heat approximately 1 inch (2.5 cm) of both rods at the same time.

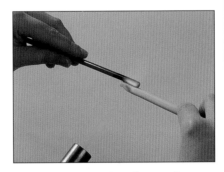

Lay one end over the other, as if you were putting toothpaste on a toothbrush, and heat the overlapped area to a molten ball. Make sure your hands are always rotating in tandem to keep the rods from twisting.

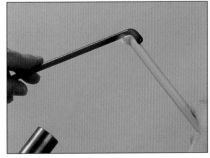

After heating each end, bend the top color down to "catch" the bottom rod;

Top: Kimberley Adams, tabular bead, 2.2 x 2.8 cm; cylinder, 2.2 cm long; bicone, 4 cm long; all decorated with twisties

Photograph: Evan Bracken

Center: Patricia Sage, *Goddess Triangle*, twistie edge decoration, 4.4 x 4.3 cm

Photograph: Evan Bracken

Bottom: Char Eagleton, twistie-decorated teapot, 3.9 cm high

Photograph: Evan Bracken

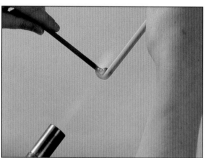

then bend the bottom rod up on the other side to catch the top rod.

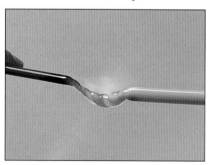

Continue heating without twisting until your dual-colored ball in the center is nicely glowing. At this point, come out of the flame and twist as quickly as possible. Make sure your hands are twisting in opposite directions. Depending on the size of the ball, how hot the glass is, and how quickly you twist, you can get up to a foot (30.5 cm) or more of twistie. You may want to tip up the thicker side of the ball to help gain control. Twisties are indispensable for bead decorating.

To achieve different effects, try twisting at different speeds and experiment with several different color combinations—opaques and transparents, filigrani, etc. Twist clear glass with an opaque color to produce another interesting look. Three or more colors can make beautiful twisties; try using a clear rod with one or two colors.

COMPLEX TWISTIES

Beads, as a rule, don't have much surface area on which to express yourself, so any compound elements you can make ahead of time will aid the process. Complex twisties have even more detail than regular twisties.

Start by heating a fairly large ball of hot glass on the end of a rod. (White is a good color with which to start because other colors show well against it.) Tip the glass rod up into the flame as you heat it until the hot glass forms a good-sized ball.

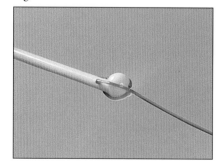

Then use your stringer to draw horizontal stripes on the ball.

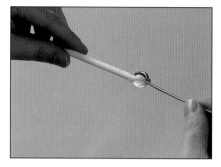

Don't worry too much about perfection at first; that will come with practice. Apply stringer in two or three colors to make a complex design. Once the ball is striped, place the glass rod in your dominant hand and grasp the very tip of the striped ball with needle-nose pliers.

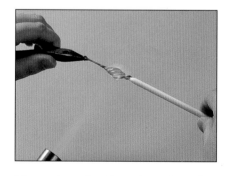

Now twist and pull a stringer from the striped ball.

An alternate method is to fuse another glass rod onto the tip of the ball of glass (make sure the rod attaches to *all* of the stripes so that they all twist) and use your two glass rods as handles. Come out of the flame and pull while

Patricia Sage, *Frog Necklace*, several accent beads with twisties, 3.8 x 2.5 cm (frog)

Photograph: Darol Strieb

twisting your hands in opposite directions. This gives a much finer twist pattern than in simple twisties.

USING TWISTIES TO MAKE AND DECORATE BEADS

Twisties can be used much like stringer to decorate your beads, but they give a more complex pattern. Twisties can be used as a trail, an end cap, or even for dots.

To add a twistie to your bead as a decorative element, keep the bead out of the flame and heat the last ½ inch (1.3 cm) of the twistie.

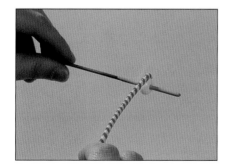

When the end of the twistie starts to droop, let it fall onto the bead. Keep moving the flame along the twistie as you rotate the mandrel, applying the twistie to the bead in short segments at a time. To avoid losing detail, try not to pull and stretch the twistie as you apply it.

If desired, you can tighten the twist by rolling the twistie as you apply it to the bead. (Be sure you roll it the right way, or you could inadvertently untwist your twistie!) When used like stringer to apply dots, a twistie forms a two-color dot in one step. This creates two side-by-side dots, not a dot on top of a dot.

Twisties are usually applied over a core bead so that you don't waste them by building up a large mass when only the surface is seen. However, twisties also can be used to make one layer of your core bead for an interesting effect. If you apply a clear or light transparent color over the decorated core, the twistie will look magnified.

There are endless combinations; for example, two filigrana rods twisted together look like a delicate chain when applied over a contrasting core bead. Try adding a twistie trail and raking it for a new look. Combine dots and twisties. Once you start mixing colors and techniques, there's no stopping you!

Cindy Jenkins, assortment of twisties and stringer

Photograph: Evan Bracken

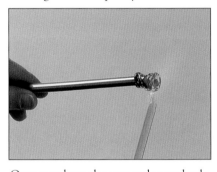

Far left: Leah Fairbanks, floral disk beads, cased stringer, .6 x 3.8 cm (typical)

Photograph: George Post

Left: Carolyn Noga, cased aventurine face with latticino hair, 2.9 x 3.5 cm

Photograph: Evan Bracken

MAKING YOUR OWN FILIGRANA & CASED STRINGER

Filigrana is a rod with a colored core encased in clear glass. When you pull it out and use it as a stringer, it gives the appearance of a much thinner rod than it really is because your eye tends to see only the colorful core.

There are many reasons to learn to case glass rods yourself and pull them into stringer. First, there is a very limited color palette of premade filigrana available. Second, commercial filigrana is always cased in clear glass, never a transparent color. Having control over this design element greatly increases the number of colors available to you, and custom-made cased stringer adds a depth and definition to your work that you can't get with ordinary stringer. No matter how close together the cased stringer is applied, the casing layer maintains a separation between the lines of color and keeps them from bleeding together into one large mass. This allows you to lay the stringer in a tight spiral to create a rosette without making just one big dot. The same goes for trails and stripes.

BASIC CASED STRINGER

To make a cased stringer, choose your core and casing color. In most instances, the casing color will be clear or transparent. Start by making a ball of glass from your casing color.

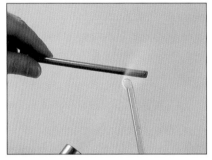

Once you have a nice-sized ball and it's glowing well, hold it in the flame. Now use your other hand to introduce the core rod into the flame, holding it above your glowing ball of casing glass. Warm about ¾ inch (2 cm) of your core rod by passing it back and forth through the flame. You want the core just hot enough so that it won't be shocked when adding the molten casing color.

With the core rod fairly cold and stiff and the casing rod gathered up into a very hot ball, wind your casing color around the core rod. Start winding at about ½ inch (1.5 cm) from the tip of your core rod and continue winding the casing glass around the core rod until the core rod is covered to its tip. Keep the core rod beneath the flame and the casing rod *in* the flame so that the core

rod doesn't start to droop and get out of control. This method also ensures that you will have an adequate supply of hot glass to complete your wind.

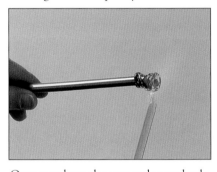

Once you have the core rod completely wound with the casing color, melt and pull off the rest of the casing rod. Now continue to heat the cased rod until any creases in the casing color start to flow together.

I like to use bead flatteners to keep everything under control (a trick I learned from Dinah Hulet).

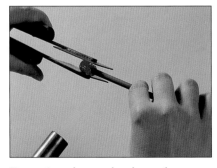

Every time the cased rod gets droopy and out of control, come out of the

64

flame and use your flatteners to squeeze it gently all the way around until it comes back into alignment and stiffens a bit.

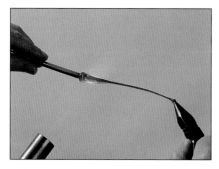

When your cased rod is symmetrical and well shaped, grasp the end with needle-nose pliers and pull the cased stringer. Remember to keep the thicker part of the cased rod in the flame as you pull the stringer.

If you use this method to case a rod with an opaque color, you will no longer have a cased stringer, but the very simplest patterned cane. Pull it a little thicker than stringer and nip it into slices ⅛ inch (3 mm) thick or less. You now have bull's eyes, or haloed dots, that can be applied to your bead with tweezers. (See Millefiori, page 78.)

BLACK STRINGER
If you've tried pulling any Effetre black rod into stringer and using it over a pale color, you may have discovered that it isn't black at all, but a very dense transparent purple. When the rod is stretched out into a thin stringer and applied to a light-colored bead, the fact that it's purple and not black is very obvious. Since black and white is such a necessary color combination, this situation can be frustrating.

For this, beadmaker Kate Fowle has come to the rescue.

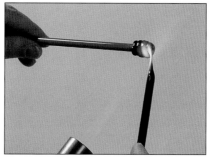

Her solution is to take an opaque dark cobalt blue rod and case it with black.

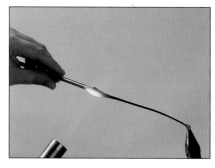

When pulled out into a stringer, no light can shine through because of the dark opaque core. This keeps the black looking black!

Why didn't I think of that?

CASED AVENTURINE STRINGER

Aventurine, also called goldstone, is a super-saturated solution of copper particles in a clear or very light transparent glass matrix. Bits of aventurine can be added to your beads, and filigrana with an aventurine core is commercially available; however, when you pull aventurine filigrana into stringer, the copper particles become farther apart, causing the glistening core to lose

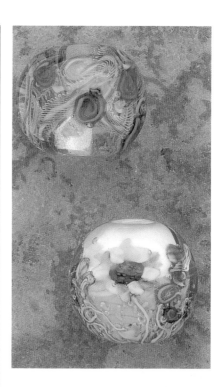

Top: Leah Fairbanks, *Rose Bead* and *Garden Bead*, cased stringer florets and stems, 2.5 cm dia.

Photograph: George Post

Bottom: Jacqueline Mixon, *Hearts & Roses*, flowers made with cased stringer, 4 x 3.2 cm

Photograph: Evan Bracken

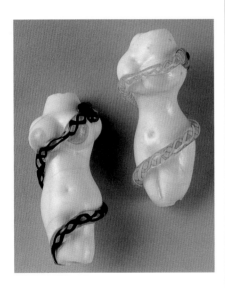

Top: Susan Simonds, *Fantasy Garden*, latticino, 3.7 x 2.9 cm

Photograph: Evan Bracken

Center: Leah Fairbanks, *Purple Trumpet Flowers*, cased stringer, 4.4 cm long

Photograph: George Post

Bottom: G. G. Havens, *Eve 2* (left) and *Eve 1* (right) with latticino snakes, 3 cm high

Photograph: Evan Bracken

much of its intensity and luster. In order to have really brilliant aventurine stringer, you need to make it yourself.

Start by breaking off a small chunk of aventurine, about the size of a pea for your first attempt.

Heat up the end of a clear rod until you have a nice glow and use the heated end to pick up the aventurine chunk.

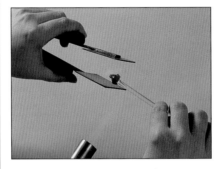

Now heat the aventurine and use your flatteners to shape it.

When the aventurine looks like an extension of your clear rod, completely case it with another rod of clear glass.

Then pull it out into a bright sparkling stringer.

In addition to using clear glass, you can case aventurine with other transparent colors. Cool colors tend to tone down the gold sparkles, and light amber intensifies them. Transparent pink casing is gorgeous. Experiment and keep a library of samples, together with descriptions of what colors were used, for future reference.

HOT **TIP**

PINK TRANSPARENT ROD MADE BY EFFETRE IS ACTUALLY A CASED ROD. BECAUSE PINK GLASS IS SO EXPENSIVE TO PRODUCE, THE CORE OF THE ROD IS CLEAR AND THE CASING IS PINK. THE THICKNESS OF THE CASING VARIES; IF IT'S NOT TOO THICK, I SOMETIMES NIP SMALL SLICES FROM THE ROD AND APPLY THEM TO MY BEAD AS IF THEY WERE PATTERN SLICES. THESE SLICES FORM DOTS THAT HAVE A CLEAR CENTER AND A PINK HALO. WHEN DRAGGED DOWN AT THE TOP AND BOTTOM, THEY MAKE SMALL HEARTS WITH PINK OUTLINES.

Right: Leah Fairbanks, *Amber Floral Bead*, complex latticino, 3.2 x 1.9 cm

Photograph: George Post

Far right: Susan Simonds (standing left), *Fantasy Garden*, 3.5 x 2.8 cm; Susan Simonds (standing right), *Fantasy Garden*, 3.5 x 2.4 cm; Pati Walton, bicone, 5 cm long; all latticino beads

Photograph: Evan Bracken

LATTICINO

Latticino, sometimes called cased twistie, is a beautiful decorative element with lots of possibilities. For your first attempt, start with a white rod so that your design will have good definition. Heat a ball of white glass and squash it into a lollipop, either with your flatteners or with a marver and paddle.

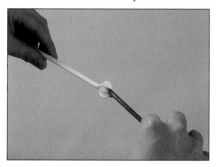

Now put a stripe of a deep transparent color in the middle of one side and the same or a contrasting deep transparent color on the other.

Apply clear stripes on both sides of each colored stripe as if you were making a double-sided striped stringer.

Finally, add a clear stripe over both colored stripes and over the white sides of the paddle so that there is a complete layer of clear glass over the entire core. (If desired, this last step can be deleted for a different effect.) Alternately heat the entire mass and use your flatteners to shape it into a cylinder. Keep heating and shaping to make a smooth, uniform cylinder-shaped end. Then grasp the end with pliers or fuse another glass rod to it to use as a handle.

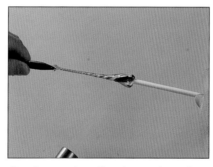

Simultaneously pull and twist the molten end to create a beautiful latticino.

For different effects, try other combinations of core colors. A black core with filigrana striped over it is very dramatic, and opaque stripes form very colorful twists.

LACY LATTICINO

This is a wonderful technique that I learned from Tom Holland. Begin with a large ball of hot clear glass and use your flatteners to form a thick cylinder.

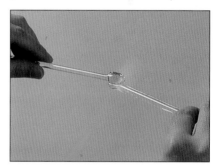

Add four stripes of clear glass along the length of the cylinder, evenly spacing the stripes all the way around.

Using a small flattener, squeeze the stripes gently into fairly tall fins. Now add a stripe of contrasting color to the channels between the fins, but make sure the clear fins are taller than the colored glass filler.

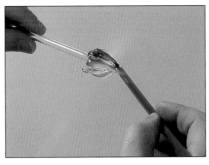

Bring the lines of color all the way to the center at the front end of your cylinder, using a rake or pick if necessary.

Now heat a second clear rod and press the hot end against a marver to flatten and slightly enlarge the end.

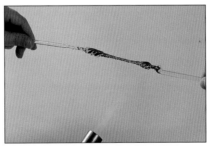

Press the flattened clear end onto the front of the striped cylinder so that it contracts all the colored lines; then heat the striped middle thoroughly until you can pull and twist it out. You will now have an entire network of interwoven lines, all nicely separated by the clear spacers.

COMBING, FEATHERING, SIDE-SHIFTING & FURROWING

COMBING & FEATHERING

Once you've mastered putting a spiral trail onto a bead, your next step is to change the look of the trail by pulling and distorting it with a tool, such as the bead rake. Combing and feathering are raking techniques, but instead of pulling the hot glass around the equator, you will drag it from side to side along the length of the bead.

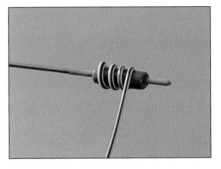

Make a long cylindrical bead and wind stringer around it several times to form a spiral trail.

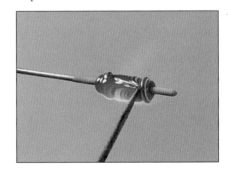

Heat one side of the trailed bead until it is glowing; then come out of the flame and touch the rake to one edge of the bead. Drag the rake to the other edge, pulling the trail as you go. As you manipulate the bead, hold it out of the flame so that the rake easily detaches from the glass. If the tool itself gets too hot, it will stick to the bead. Should this happen, stay out of the flame, blow on the rake, wait a few seconds, and wiggle the rake slightly until it comes loose. (The metal rake cools and shrinks more quickly than the glass, which allows it to release.) Dip the rake into a cup of water after each pull to keep it from heating up and sticking during the next use.

HOT TIP

DON'T DIG THE RAKE INTO THE BODY OF THE BEAD, OR YOU WILL PULL TOO MUCH GLASS AND DISTORT THE SHAPE OR POSSIBLY PULL THE BEAD LOOSE FROM THE MANDREL. REMEMBER, YOU'RE TRYING TO RAKE ONLY THE TRAIL, WHICH IS ON THE SURFACE OF THE BEAD.

Heat the next side and rake it just as you did the first. Continue to rake your bead all the way around, dipping the bead rake in water each time. I like to alternate directions with each stroke of the rake, but you must plan for this in order to obtain an even number of strokes.

HOT TIP

SOMETIMES IT'S EASIER TO RAKE YOUR PATTERN THREE OR FOUR TIMES IN ONE DIRECTION, WIDELY SPACING THE STROKES, AND THEN GO BACK AND RAKE THE OPPOSITE DIRECTION IN BETWEEN.

Because dragging the glass from one side to the other will change the shape of your bead somewhat, you most likely will need to reheat and marver your bead back into the desired shape. If you rake very evenly, the resulting shape can be quite pleasing without

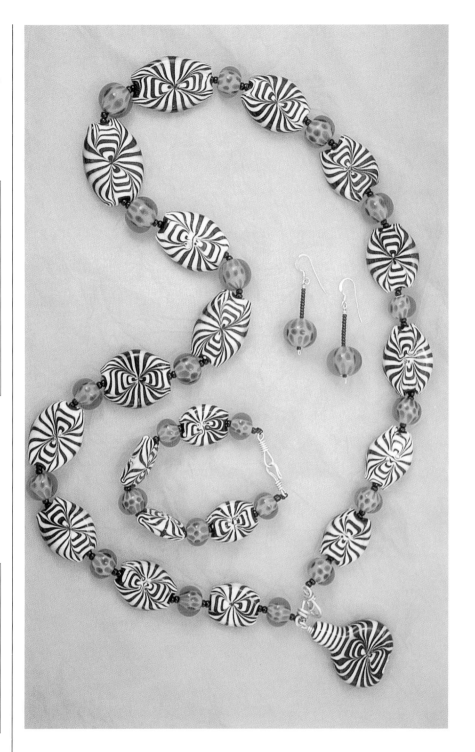

Tom Holland, spider-combed necklace, bracelet, and earrings, 5.1 x 3.8 cm (largest)

Photograph: Tom Holland

69

Patricia Frantz (left and right), two side-shifted bicones, 3.8 cm long (larger); Lorraine Yamaguchi (center), combing, 2.3 x 2.8 cm

Photograph: Evan Bracken

Tom Holland (left), combed tabular bead, 4.1 x 2.7 cm; Tom Boylan (center), swirl dot bead with side-shifted ends, 4 cm long; Tom Holland (right), furrowed bicone, 3.7 cm long

Photograph: Evan Bracken

reshaping. Some experienced beadmakers prefer using a cold stringer in place of a metal tool to rake their beads. Because the stringer can easily be melted or broken, this method requires more expertise as well as a firm grasp of heat control.

HOT TIP

Most glassworkers use the terms combing and feathering interchangeably for this process of raking a spiral trail. According to Tom Holland, who has researched these methods extensively, when you *feather* a bead, you pull back and forth across the trail *without* lifting your tool or stringer to change directions, thus creating one long trail that loops back and forth. In *combing*, each pull is separate, creating a slightly different look.

SIDE-SHIFTING

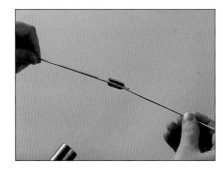

For this technique, make another long cylinder and apply your stringer in parallel lines placed horizontally across the bead. Manipulate these lines either with the sharp edge of a graphite paddle or with the blade of a knife.

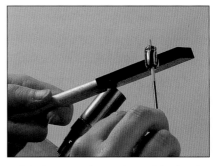

While keeping the surface of the bead hot enough to move, hold the tool firmly against the bead, perpendicular to the stripes, and rotate the bead, pressing hard enough to distort the lines. Now heat the next section, place your tool against it, and rotate the bead in the opposite direction.

Continue this process until you've covered the entire surface of the bead, creating a herringbone pattern. An uneven number

Kristina Logan, assortment of beads with poked dots, simple dots, and twisted dots, 5.1 cm long (largest green bead)

Photograph: Dean Powel

of strokes looks more balanced; try three at first for ease.

For more of a spiral shift instead of the zigzag herringbone pattern, try heating the whole bead and quickly using your tool to push just the ends of the bead in opposite directions.

FURROWING

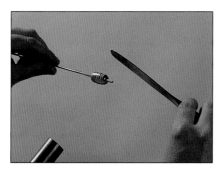

Furrowing is somewhat similar to the side-shifting process, except that the stringer is trailed on in a spiral, as it is for the combing and feathering techniques. Using the entire edge of a knife, contact and push the stripes in one direction all at once.

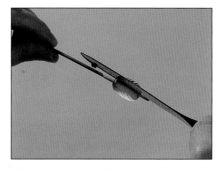

This leaves the trails separate from each other and creates a herringbone pattern.

Cindy Jenkins, feathering (left), 2.6 cm long; furrowing (center), 2.4 x 1.8 cm; side-shifting (right), 2.4 cm long

Photograph: Evan Bracken

PINCHING, POKING, SNIPPING & PLUNGING

PINCHING & POKING

Beads can be shaped using many different tools in addition to your marver. While hot, beads can be poked with metal, ceramic, and graphite objects to create dents and furrows in select places.

Look around and see what objects you already have that could be used as tools, keeping in mind that anything you use might get ruined. Pliers are common household tools that can be used to pinch, pull, and texture your beads.

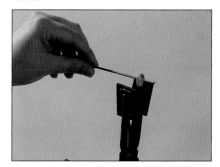

Lampworking pliers with leaf vein designs are available to make your beads look more special. These aren't a necessity, but they produce very inter-

Top left: Mary Klotz, pinched leaves, 2.3 x 4.6 cm (largest); Sue Richers Elgar, pinched amber pendant bead, 2.4 x 1.5 cm

Photograph: Evan Bracken

Top right: Lavana Shurtliff (top), lavender bead with poked and cased dots, 2.6 x 1.9 cm; Kristen Frantzen Orr, four floral beads: *Spring Garden* (left), 1.8 cm dia.; *Little Pink Lilies* (upper center), 1.6 cm dia.; *Garden at Dawn* (lower center), 2 cm dia.; *Wildflower Cylinder* (right), 2.8 cm long; all with poked and cased dots

Photograph: Evan Bracken

Center: Pati Walton, *Calla Lily Garden*, floral plunge, 3.8 x 3.2 cm

Photograph: Mike Bush

Bottom: Audrie Wiesenfelder, *Butterscotch Butterfly*, pinched, 3.8 x 1.6 cm

Photograph: Tom Van Eynde

esting beads. Remember to reheat any area that you shape with a cold tool; the chilled portion can crack off the hot bead if you don't balance the heat in the entire bead.

SNIPPING

Regular scissors can be used to snip your bead for a special effect.

Wind a thin, disk-shaped bead and snip it in several places around the equator.

Pinching these snipped parts produces a flowerlike bead. Be careful not to

snip too close to the center of the bead; this can pull the bead loose from the mandrel, and you won't be able to finish working on it. A pair of scissors with sharp, thin blades works best.

PLUNGING

Another fun technique is to add a transparent dot of glass over a spot that has been poked or *plunged* into the bead.

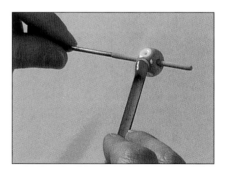

This process traps a tiny air bubble within your bead, which can be seen through the transparent area.

Patricia Sage has developed a sophisticated variation that she calls the *floral plunge*. Make a thick bead using clear glass or a transparent color and add dots around one or more central points.

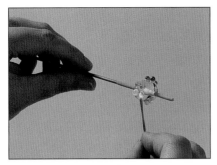

For greater depth, add more transparent dots over the first set.

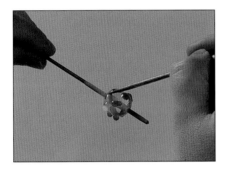

Raking the dots outward to make them more pointed further enhances the depth.

Make as many of these dot clusters as you'd like on the surface of the bead.

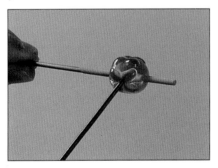

Super-heat the center of the first group of dots and plunge a tungsten pick straight down into the center. This pushes the inside edges of the colored dots down into the base and creates a three-dimensional appearance.

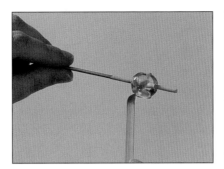

Using a light transparent color, add a dot of glass over the plunged hole.

In place of a tungsten pick, you can use a sturdy cold stringer to make the center hole. This leaves a stringer line down to the bottom of the flower. For an even more realistic effect, bundle three to five filigrana rods together; then heat and pull them into a single stringer. Using this for the plunger leaves behind stamenlike threads in the center of the flower. These flowers look much more lifelike than those simply applied to the outside of a bead.

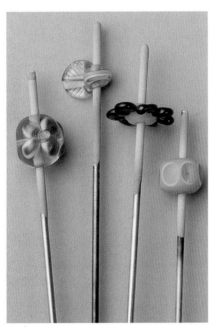

Cindy Jenkins, left to right: floral plunge, 1.8 x 1.6 cm; pinched, 1.4 x 1.8 cm; snipped, .6 x 2.3 cm; poked, 1.1 x 1.5 cm

Photograph: Evan Bracken

Top: Patricia Sage, floral plunge bead, 1.3 x 3.5 cm

Photograph: Evan Bracken

Center: Karen Ovington, *Fish Totem*, pinched fins, 4.4 cm long

Photograph: Evan Bracken

Bottom: Kristina Logan, amber barrel bead with poked dots, 3.2 x 3.2 cm

Photograph: Dean Powel

ADDING METALS

METAL FOIL

Even the plainest bead becomes memorable with the addition of a little silver or gold. Silver foil is a good material with which to start, since it's fairly inexpensive and easy to use. Foil is about five times thicker than leaf and therefore more manageable. While leaf is difficult just to get out of the package, foil can actually be picked up and handled with your fingers, and it can be cut with normal scissors.

To start, cut off a strip that will wrap all the way around your bead—too much is better than not enough.

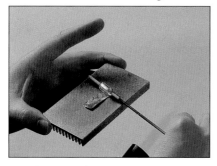

Lay the strip of silver foil on your marver and set it aside while you make a core bead. Heat the bead until it has a nice glow; then roll it over the foil. If your bead isn't hot enough, it simply will not pick up the foil. No harm done—just reheat the bead and try again. Keep rolling until all of the foil is wrapped around the bead. Don't worry if it overlaps.

Before returning to the flame, use a metal tool, such as the side of your bead rake, to burnish the foil firmly onto the glass. This removes any air pockets and makes the foil less likely to burn off.

If desired, cover the bead with a layer of clear or transparent colored glass so that the foil can show through. While heating and adding the casing color, try not to expose the silver-covered core bead to any more flame than absolutely necessary to keep it warm. If too much heat is applied, the silver will eventually disappear.

If you wish to leave the silver exposed on the surface of the bead, heat it just enough to allow it to flow and adhere to the bead. Move the bead in and out of the flame while turning it to keep the silver from burning off.

SOLID METAL

Fine silver wire or shavings also can be used to decorate your bead. Because wire is thicker than foil, it tends to ball up on the surface of the bead and create discrete areas of silver over the surface of the bead.

GOLD LEAF

Gold foil would be easier to use than gold leaf, but gold foil is quite expensive. Since gold withstands the heat better than silver, the leaf does just fine. The most difficult part of working with gold leaf is getting it out of the package and onto your marver so that you can pick it up with your hot bead. This method is a combination of tricks I learned from Jana Burnham and Tom Holland.

Gold leaf comes in a package of 25 ultra-thin sheets. Between each sheet is a piece of rouge paper, which doesn't adhere to the gold leaf.

Right: Brian Kerkvliet, turquoise barrel bead with silver foil spiral wrap, 2.7 x 1.8 cm

Photograph: Evan Bracken

Far right: René Roberts, three barrel beads and one stone-shaped bead, gold leaf, 3.3 x 1.8 cm (largest barrel bead)

Photograph: Evan Bracken

Carefully fold back the rouge paper and expose one side of the first sheet of gold leaf. Avoid creating any breeze or disturbance; the slightest movement can cause the sheet to wrinkle up or even blow away. Lay a piece of notebook or typing paper slightly larger than the leaf on top of the exposed sheet. Turn over the entire book and expose the other side of the same sheet of gold leaf by opening the book from the opposite side. Slip another piece of paper on top of the back side of the leaf. You now have the gold leaf sandwiched between two pieces of paper and can slip it out of the book.

Now that the leaf is protected, you can use scissors to cut strips or squares from

the sheet. If you touch the leaf with your fingers, it will stick to your skin and be nearly impossible to remove.

To make a tool for manipulating the gold leaf, pull out the first sheet of rouge paper from your package, cut it into strips, and roll the strips into toothpicklike cylinders with your fingers.

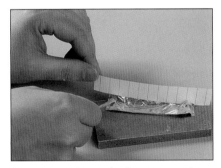

You can use these cylinders to tease the gold leaf from its paper sandwich and get it onto your marver. Don't worry if you tear or wrinkle the leaf; it will still work just fine. Lay a small strip of paper on top of the gold leaf to keep it from blowing away while you make your bead.

Once you're ready, simply roll your hot bead on top of the gold leaf to pick it

up onto the surface of your bead. You can leave the gold exposed on the surface if you like. Just heat the gold until you see it become a bit shiny and flow over the bead surface. The more you heat the gold, the more the pattern will crackle and break up. Completely or partially cover the gold with transparent glass if you want greater depth.

PALLADIUM LEAF

Palladium holds up to the flame much better than silver, and palladium leaf is used exactly as gold leaf is. The effect is quite different, however. Palladium looks silvery when you start, but changes to different shades, depending on its level of heat exposure. Blue, gray, teal, and green are just some of the colors you may see. Because of the amount of heat involved in casing, palladium generally will look silver when encased. Its other colors are developed at temperatures lower than those normally required for casing. Although palladium isn't as predictable as gold and silver, you can get some interesting effects by playing with it.

METAL TUBING

Winding a clear or light-colored transparent bead around a piece of copper tubing creates a beautiful effect. (Hazel Teefy gave me this idea.) The copper reacts to the heat, turning a deep burgundy color with a subtle sheen.

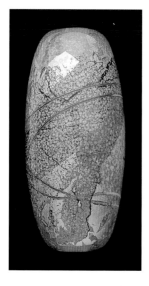

HOT TIP

THE EASIEST WAY TO CUT COPPER TUBING WITHOUT CRIMPING IT IS TO USE A CRAFT KNIFE. ROLL THE TUBING BACK AND FORTH UNDER THE KNIFE, ALLOWING THE BLADE TO CREATE A FURROW IN THE TUBE. USE YOUR FINGERS OR PLIERS (GENTLY!) TO BREAK THE TUBE APART. BEND AWAY FROM THE SCORED SIDE, SINCE YOU'RE TRYING TO POP OPEN THAT FURROW.

I've found that ⁵⁄₃₂-inch (4 mm) copper tubing and ³⁄₃₂-inch (2.4 mm) mandrels work well for this process. After preparing the mandrel with separator as usual, cut the copper tubing slightly shorter than you want your finished bead to be.

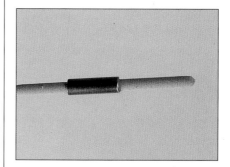

Slip the copper tubing section onto your mandrel so that the separator extends beyond both sides of the tubing. Heat your glass rod as usual; then, just before you're ready to apply the glass, heat the copper tubing on the mandrel.

Top left: René Roberts, *Atlantis Series,* gold leaf, 4.4 x 1.9 cm

Photograph: George Post

Top right: Stevi Belle (far left), *Asteroid,* 6 x 3.8 cm; Stevi Belle (top), *Asteroid,* gold leaf, 5.6 x 3 cm, both with gold and silver leaf and silver wire; Inara Knight (bottom), two long bicones accented with gold leaf and silver wire, 4.5 cm long

Photograph: Evan Bracken

Center left: Mary Klotz, six copper core beads, 1.2 x .5 cm

Photograph: Evan Bracken

Center right: Audrie Wiesenfelder, cobalt blue tabular bead with silver foil and wire, 3.8 x 3.6 cm

Photograph: Tom Van Eynde

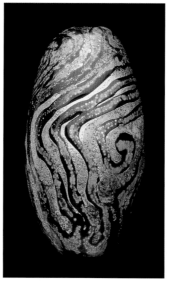

Bottom: René Roberts, *Moss Series,* gold leaf, 4.4 x 1.3 cm

Photograph: George Post

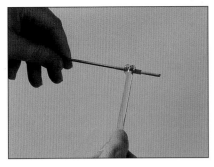

When the copper has a glow, start adding glass. The trick is to apply the glass in such a way that it sticks to both the mandrel and the copper tubing. This stabilizes the tube and keeps it from spinning while you finish covering it with glass. By extending the glass slightly over the ends of the tubing on both sides, your bead will have smooth glass ends instead of sharp metal ones.

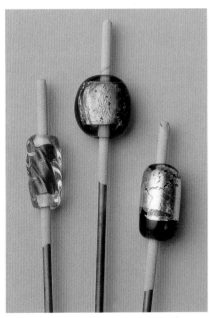

Cindy Jenkins, copper tube (left), 2 cm long; silver foil (center), 1.7 x 1.7 cm; gold leaf (right), 2 cm long

Photograph: Evan Bracken

INCLUSIONS AND SURFACE TREATMENTS

There are many different materials that can be used to enhance the surface of your beads. In addition to frit, which is simply bits of ground glass, other granules and powders adhere readily to hot glass. In fact, whatever crumbs come in contact with the hot surface of your bead will be picked up and held there, whether you intended them to or not. For this reason, it's important that all of your tools stay clean.

Here are some materials that can be used to enhance your other decorating techniques.

MICA

Mica is an inert organic substance that somewhat resembles glitter. Because mica doesn't actually melt at bead-making temperatures, it works better when used sparingly and trapped between layers of glass. When applied this way, mica produces glittering speckles that are magnified by the transparent layer above.

LUSTER POWDERS

Also known as pixie dust and pearlescent powders, these are very fine talc-like powders. They come in many colors and are rolled onto the surface of the hot bead. Depending upon the effect you want to achieve, luster powders can be left on the surface or encased.

ENAMEL POWDER

Enamel powder is a special type of finely ground colored glass. One good reason to work with enamel is to increase your available color palette. A thin layer of enamel on the surface of your bead can intensify an existing color or create a new color, and a light dusting produces a speckled effect.

Top: Karen Ovington, hollow bead with frit and powders on the surface, 3 x 2 cm

Photograph: Tom Van Eynde

Bottom: Stevi Belle, *Ancient Purple Vessel* (left), 7.6 x 3 cm; and *Spiraling Cylinder* (right), 5.7 x 2.2 cm; both with powders, frit, and other surface treatments

Photograph: Evan Bracken

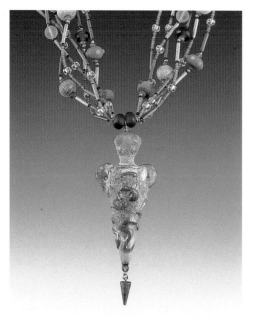

Left: Stevi Belle and Audrey Forcier, *Ancient Green Necklace*, powders and frit, 7.6 x 3.2 cm (largest)
Photograph: Jerry Anthony

Above: Jana Burnham, faceted beads with metallic powders, 6.4 cm dia. (typical)
Photograph: Ralph Gabriner

Enamels melt but don't really blend into each other. If you mix blue and yellow enamels, you won't get green; instead, you'll get tiny individual specks of blue and yellow. Casing magnifies this effect, opening up a treasure trove of decorating ideas. Because an enamel creates such a thin color layer over the core bead (unlike casing with a glass rod), you can use an engraving tool to cut through the enamel to the core bead for a two-toned design. This "cold-working" method allows you to put letters, symbols, lines, squiggles—anything you like—on the surface of the bead.

Enamel powder used as a casing layer creates a very thin coating, which allows you to get outline detail that's impossible with regular glass rod. For example, if you roll white glass in red enamel powder, then insert it into a heart mold, you will create a white heart center with a thin red outline. After casing the heart with another color, the thin red layer will appear as a very delicate line in the overall design.

COMMERCIAL MILLEFIORI

Effetre produces an extensive line of pattern slices called *millefiori*. (The term for a single slice is *millefiore*.) The word means "thousand flowers" in Italian, and you've probably seen millefiori in paperweights and other decorative items. They're handmade in the Effetre factory in Italy, where they are cut from glass canes.

The canes from which millefiori are cut are first produced in a fairly large format. Using many layers of colored rods and molded shapes, detailed patterns are built up to create flowers, stars, hearts, bull's eyes, etc. Each large pattern assembly is thoroughly heated in a glass blower's furnace and then stretched out into a long, thin cane. As the glass is stretched, the pattern stays the same in every detail but becomes miniaturized. Then the cane is cut into slices approximately ⅛ inch (3 mm) thick. Each slice reveals a tiny pattern in cross-section and is a miniature work of art. Adding these to your beads gives them an intriguingly complex appearance that you can't get any other way.

Luster powders (top right), enamel powders (top left), mica (bottom)

To start, lay as many millefiori as you want on your marver. Unless you have a hot plate or electric frying pan to preheat them, it's not a good idea to use millefiori much larger than ⅛ inch (3 mm) in any dimension. The sudden shock, when the cold glass touches the hot bead, may crack the millefiori.

Make your core bead as large as you want; then heat one area until it's glowing. If the surface isn't hot enough, the millefiore won't stick.

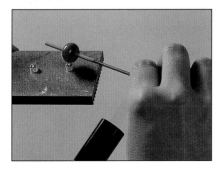

Now press the hot spot straight down onto the millefiore, picking it up, and immediately return the bead to the flame. When the entire millefiore slice is hot, press the bead straight down onto your marver or graphite paddle, using firm and even pressure to push the millefiore into the bead. Be careful not to push sideways, as this may smear the millefiore. Continue to pick up more millefiori, returning to the flame each time, until you have as many as you want on the bead. Use the marver or paddle as necessary to shape your bead.

For more precise placement of millefiori, you can use tweezers to add them directly onto the hot glowing portions of your bead.

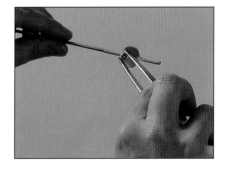

This is easier if you preheat the millefiori on a hot plate or the shelf of your torch marver, if you have one. If not, you'll need to warm them by holding them with the tweezers and passing them quickly through your flame a few times. The trick is to heat them

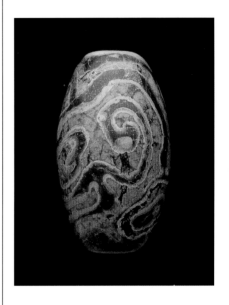

Top left: Pati Walton, *Dolphin Bead*, commercial millefiori on the ocean floor beneath the handmade dolphin, 3.8 x 3.2 cm

Photograph: Mike Bush

Top center: David Vogt, torso, luster powders, 3 x 1.5 cm

Photograph: Evan Bracken

Top right: Kate Fowle, "stone" beads with enamel powders, gold, and handmade millefiori, 3 x 1.7 cm

Photograph: Evan Bracken

Bottom: René Roberts, *Stonework Series*, metal colorants, 3.8 x 1.9 cm

Photograph: George Post

G. G. Havens, *Goldfish*, pinched tails,
1.9 x 3.4 cm; Jacob Fishman, bug,
pinched wings, 1.7 x 2.9 cm

Photograph: Evan Bracken

HOT TIP

enough so that they don't break from thermal shock when applied, but not so much that they stick to the tweezers.

When working with Effetre millefiori that contain white glass, don't move the bead in and out of the flame for shaping. The process of repeatedly chilling and reheating allows crystals to grow and makes the white portions of the millefiori lose their shiny (glassy) surface. This crystallization of the glass is called *devitrification* and is caused by holding the millefiore slices just below the temperature at which they are liquid (the *liquidus* point).

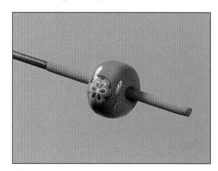

If your millefiori do lose their shiny, glassy look, put the bead back in the flame and reheat it until the surface completely liquefies and the millefiori "reglaze" themselves. Once this occurs, come out of the flame and stay out.

Try not to let your millefiori cool to the point of devitrification. Apply the millefiori, heat your bead thoroughly,

then stop. Even though the glass can be reglazed, the pattern tends to "bloom" and lose some of its crisp definition.

Some glass formulas are particularly susceptible to devitrification, and apparently this is the case with the white glass used in millefiori and in the cores of most filigrana rods—not white glass in general. If you plan to do some extra shaping, you can avoid this problem by quickly encasing each millefiore with a dollop of clear glass, thus protecting it from devitrification. The clear casing somewhat magnifies the design, creating a paperweight effect. Another way to avoid devitrification is to use only millefiori with no white in them, but this is a limited solution, since most millefiori contain some white.

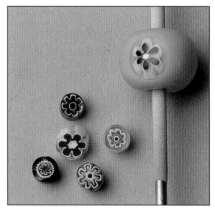

Cindy Jenkins, assorted millefiori and bead with applied millefiore, 1.1 x 1.5 cm

Photograph: Evan Bracken

ADVANCED TECHNIQUES

Inara Knight, *Lightshades Necklace*, dichroic glass, sculpted beads, 3 x 2.7 cm (typical sculpted bead)
Photograph: Evan Bracken

MAKING YOUR OWN MILLEFIORI

Sooner or later you may want to try making your own millefiori. This will not only make your beads unique, but it will also give you complete control over the colors and designs. Your white areas won't devitrify as in commercial millefiori, and you can choose a contemporary palette that is otherwise unavailable. Once you begin to think in cross section, lots of handmade pattern slices will come to mind. (See Figure 1 for several ideas.)

SIMPLE MILLEFIORI

The simplest form of millefiore is a cased rod that you pull a little thicker than a stringer. Make a cased rod and pull it to a thickness of ⅛ or ¼ inch (3 or 6 mm), depending on your preference. Cut it into sections with a rod nipper and apply the pieces just as you do commercial millefiori. A clear center produces a "window" that reveals the core bead beneath it.

WHIRLIGIG MILLEFIORI

A more interesting effect can be easily achieved just by combining a few simple techniques.

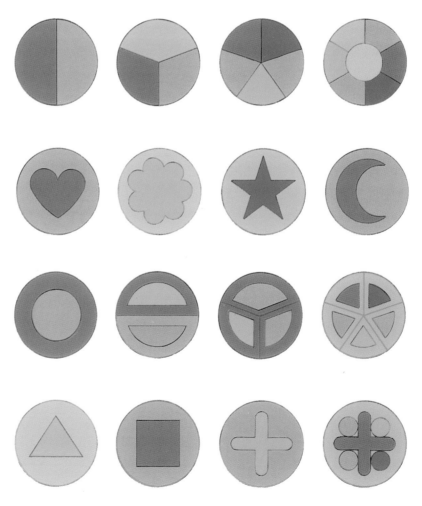

Figure 1

82

Opposite left: Don Schneider, four tube beads with hand-made millefiori, 4 x 2 cm (flat tube bead at left)
Photograph: Evan Bracken

Opposite right: Dinah Hulet, assortment of handmade millefiori, 1 cm dia. (largest)
Photograph: Evan Bracken

Right: Brian Kerkvliet, vase bead with portrait millefiore, 4.8 cm high
Photograph: Evan Bracken

Far right: Loren Stump, shell bead with hand-pulled cane dolphins, 4.9 x 3.1 cm
Photograph: Evan Bracken

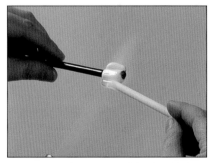

For a whirligig pattern, encase a core rod with a contrasting color; then add horizontal stripes onto the casing with another contrasting color.

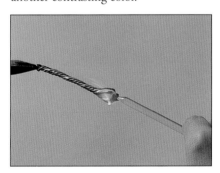

Pull it out, with or without twisting. (Remember not to pull it too thin.) When cut into slices and applied to your bead, the whirligig produces one of two possible patterns. If the cane isn't twisted while pulling, it produces a central dot surrounded by a series of straight lines (a starburst); if twisted, it makes a spiral pattern. This is an ancient Chinese cane technique that can be done in endless color combinations.

MULTICOLORED CANE

Here's another simple design. Bundle three or more contrasting rods together with masking tape; then heat and shape them into a smooth cylinder with your flatteners.

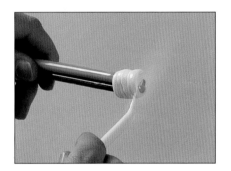

Case the bundle with another color if you wish.

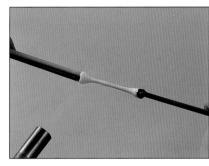

When pulled out and sliced, you'll have a simple but effective pattern. If you want to get more complex, bundle three of these pulled rods together, heat, case, and pull out again. This continues to miniaturize the parts.

SCULPTED MILLEFIORI

Now let's a make design that involves a little sculpting.

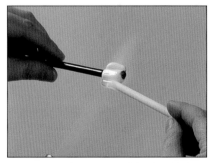

Starting with a black rod, case it with white for good contrast and add thick stripes of white on opposite sides of the cane to create an oblong shape.

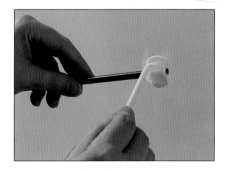

Use your paddle, flatteners, or an old knife to flatten the heated stripes; then add more white stripes to make a marquis or eye shape. When you're happy with the shape, you can case it again in black or another contrasting color if you like.

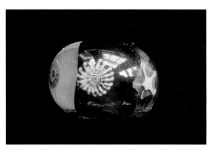

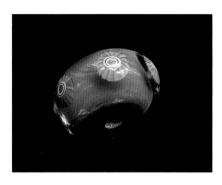

Top: Nancy Pilgrim, ocean bead with hand-pulled cane fish, 4.7 x 2.5 cm

Photograph: Evan Bracken

Center: Don Schneider, cased bead with hand-made millefiori applied to casing, 1.8 x 2.2 cm

Photograph: Bill Bresler

Bottom: Don Schneider, cased bead with hand-made millefiori applied to casing, 1.8 x 2.2 cm

Photograph: Bill Bresler

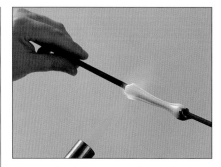

Do any final shaping, pull out the cane, and slice it with a rod nipper for use as an eye cane.

MOLD-FORMED MILLEFIORI

Also available for making millefiori are shaping tools called optic molds. These are small aluminum molds with simple designs cut into them in a tapered fashion—larger at the top and smaller at the bottom. The wide mouth allows you to get a good-sized ball of molten glass into the top of the mold, and the tapered shape makes it easy to remove your hot glass from the mold after taking the impression. When using a mold, set it on your marver because the mold itself is open at the bottom.

HOT TIP

THE HEART-SHAPED OPTIC MOLD SEEMS TO BE THE EASIEST TO USE. START WITH THAT ONE!

To use an optic mold, begin by heating a glass rod until you have a sizable ball of molten glass. (Be sure your ball of hot glass isn't too wide to fit inside the mold's opening.)

Center the glass over the opening and quickly press your glass down to the bottom of the mold. As you press the glass downward, the mold will compress it into the proper shape. You must work fairly quickly because the mold rapidly absorbs the heat from the glass, causing it to stiffen.

When you remove the glass from the mold, you will see that your molten ball of glass has been transformed into whatever shape your chosen mold produces. If you didn't get a good impression of the pattern, reheat and repeat this step as needed.

Now cover the molded shape with a contrasting color. To cover a complex shape, apply your casing color in stripes parallel with the length of the glass rod rather than winding it around, as you did when encasing your other canes. Work from the end where the molded shape attaches to the glass rod and lay your stripe lengthwise to the tip. Fill all the valleys first; then work your way around the entire shape, being careful not to let the core get so hot that the molded shape becomes distorted.

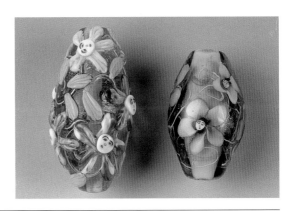

Top left: Char Eagleton, aquarium beads, fish individually applied with stringer, 4 x 2.8 cm (largest)

Photograph: Evan Bracken

Top right: Brian Kerkvliet, *Gold Dream Catcher*, handmade millefiori, 5.1 x 3.8 cm

Photograph: Brian Kerkvliet

Right: Nancy Pilgrim, two floral beads with face-cane centers, 4.5 x 2.4 cm (larger)

Photograph: Evan Bracken

Try to avoid trapping air bubbles as you encase your cane. Air pockets will leave pinpoint holes in your final design and make the pulled rod brittle and difficult to handle.

Each successive stripe of casing glass should touch the last stripe completely from one end to the other. This will enable you to stretch the cane evenly. When the molded shape is completely covered, spend some time melting and shaping the outer glass into a thick round cylinder *without* twisting the internal pattern.

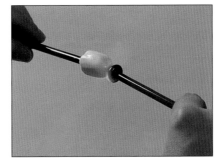

Once the cane is satisfactory, attach another glass rod to the front tip. It's important that the casing contact both rod handles in all areas so that the entire mass will pull out evenly. Prepare the second handle by heating another glass rod and pressing the hot end against a marver before attaching it to the tip of your cane. This spreads the end of the rod so that it has a greater surface area with which to pull.

Using both hands in tandem, roll and heat the central mass until it's warm enough to pull. It's likely that the rod handles, which are much thinner than the molded portion, will heat up and

HOT TIP

SOME BEADMAKERS PREFER TO USE HARD GLASS (PYREX) FOR THEIR HANDLES WHEN MAKING MOLDED MILLEFIORI BECAUSE IT MELTS AT A MUCH HIGHER TEMPERATURE THAN SOFT GLASS (EFFETRE, BULLSEYE, OR UROBOROS) AND STAYS STIFFER. THESE TWO TYPES OF GLASS ARE EXTREMELY INCOMPATIBLE, WHICH DOESN'T CAUSE A PROBLEM WHEN EVERYTHING IS HOT. AFTER COOLING, THE PYREX HANDLES WILL EASILY POP OFF. MAKE SURE YOU KEEP HARD GLASS WELL LABELED AND SEPARATE FROM YOUR STOCK OF SOFT GLASS.

Figure 2

Above: Bernadette Fuentes, aquarium bead with hand-pulled cane fish and creatures, 2.5 x 3 cm

Photograph: Tommy Elder

Right: Brian Kerkvliet, trio of beads with handmade millefiori, 2.7 x 1.3 (bicone at top)

Photograph: Evan Bracken

start to droop before the center is ready to pull. To remedy this, come out of the flame and blow on both handles near the center. Thin glass heats faster than thick glass, but it also chills faster. Blowing on the general area will therefore cool the thin attachments more than it will cool the central pattern section.

When the handles have lost their glow, lightly pull to test whether the central mass is ready. If the rods begin to stretch, stop pulling immediately. Alternately heat the center and chill the handles, doing a gentle test pull each time, until the center is ready to stretch. During the heating cycles, apply light pressure to the handles, pressing them toward the center to help maintain a firm attachment.

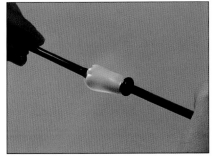

Pull the molded cane to a diameter of ¼ inch (6 mm) or a little less. When it's cool, cut thin slices with the nippers.

ALPHABET MILLEFIORI

Have you ever wanted to sign your name to a particularly precious bead, but didn't know how you could possibly manage it? You can really amaze people if you build up a library of alphabet canes. Once you have built the initial alphabet, you can bundle the letters together and pull out your initials, your name, or entire words. Glassblower Dick Marquis gained fame throughout the art glass community when he pulled the entire text of the Lord's Prayer in alphabet cane, a piece of which is now in the collection of the Corning Museum of Glass.

You might want to start with a little less ambitious project.

Figure 2 shows the suggested steps involved in assembling block-style letters and numbers. Typically, it's advisable to start in the center of the letter block and work outward in layers. The secret to succeeding with this process is to think in cross-section—to visualize the construction as a three-dimensional symbol that you will stretch and slice. Letters are more challenging than abstract shapes because if you distort the internal design very much, you will lose all of the meaning.

Start with an easy letter, such as an O or U, and work your way up to the more difficult ones. You'll probably want to combine your individual letters, so use identical or coordinated colors when building different letters. Try to pull the letters to about the same diameter so that you can bundle them into words.

If block letters aren't difficult enough for you, try cursive writing. Loren Stump is the only beadmaker I know who signs his name in script rather than in block letters. (Not to be outdone by Dick Marquis, Loren Stump has made a pictorial cane of the Last Supper. Unbelievable!)

CASED BEADS

Casing is the process of covering your core bead with a layer of clear or transparent glass to add depth and mystery to your design. You may choose to case your bead completely or to case it selectively by covering only certain areas. For ease of understanding, the casing color in these instructions is always referred to as clear, but you can substitute any transparent color when making your own beads.

Adding small dots of clear glass in strategic places on your bead magnifies whatever is underneath. This creates

Top left: Kate Fowle (left), *Fantasy Bead*, 3 x 2.1 cm; Jacqueline Mixon (second from left), *Multifloral*, 1.7 x 2.4 cm; Kate Fowle (third from left), *Fantasy Bead*, 3.4 x 2.2 cm; Kimberley Osibin (right), floral bead with pink transparent casing, 2.3 cm dia.

Photograph: Evan Bracken

Top right: Patricia Frantz (center), tiger-striped bicone with spot-cased eyes, 3.9 x 1.9 cm; Kristina Logan (left and right), two cased beads with dots applied to casing, 1.1 x 1.8 cm

Photograph: Evan Bracken

Bottom: David Vogt (left), flower pendant bead, 5.4 x 1.5 cm; David Vogt (top), flower pendant bead, 3.1 x 2.7 cm; Bernadette Fuentes (right), aquarium bead, 3.8 x 2 cm; all with heavy "paperweight" casing

Photograph: Evan Bracken

what I call a *paperweight effect* and spotlights certain design areas in your bead. Heat the end of a clear rod so that it's almost dripping; then let the molten glass flow on top of the area you wish to highlight. The bead itself should be *relatively* cool and stiff so that you don't deform the design when you add the clear spot. Of course, the bead must be warm enough so that the hot glass doesn't crack it.

If you wish to encase your core bead completely, there are several methods you can use.

THE SECRET TO GOOD CASING IS *HEAT CONTROL*. THE CASING GLASS SHOULD BE SUPER HOT, AND THE CORE BEAD SHOULD BE WARM BUT STIFF SO THAT IT DOESN'T DISTORT WHILE BEING ENCASED.

WINDING METHOD
Keep the core bead warm, but don't allow it to glow.

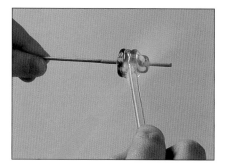

Simultaneously, heat your casing rod until it's very liquid. Treating your core bead as a thick mandrel, wind it with the casing rod. It's better to stop and start, if necessary, in order to keep the casing rod *really* hot. Trying to force an insufficiently heated casing rod over the core will trap air bubbles in your bead. Use a push-pull movement while applying the hot glass to help force out any trapped air.

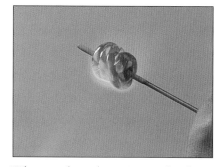

When you have the entire core bead covered, spend some time in the flame to even out the heat throughout the bead and smooth out any surface ripples.

FULL-GATHER TECHNIQUE

This method, developed by Patricia Sage, produces a thick magnifying layer over your core bead for a heavy, paperweight effect.

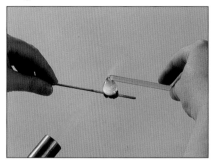

Start with a very large ball of superheated clear glass and let it literally drip over your just-warm bead to cover the surface completely. This is easier to do if you have a thick rod of clear glass; you can form a very thick rod by binding two or three clear rods together with masking tape.

When the molten ball of glass has flowed completely around the core bead, use the flame to burn off the remaining rod.

When using a single-fuel torch to put a full-gather casing on a large bead, I sometimes find that I have to case in two steps, doing one side at a time.

SHEET CASING METHOD

For those times when a thinner layer of clear glass is desirable, Patricia Sage has developed another technique she calls *sheet casing*. Again heat a large ball of clear glass, but rather than dripping it over the bead, use a flattening tool to squash the ball into a lollipop.

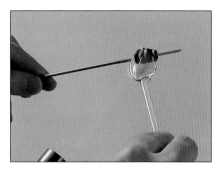

Now heat the flattened disk and wrap it around the warm core bead.

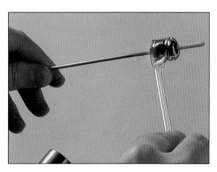

Starting at one side of the bead, wind the casing diagonally over the middle, until it meets on the other side. Afterward, you can patch any areas that are missed.

It takes practice to develop an eye for how much hot glass you will need to completely encase your bead. In general, you'll need a ball of casing glass that is about 1.5 times the size of the core bead for the full-gather method; for sheet casing, you'll need a ball approximately the same size as the core bead.

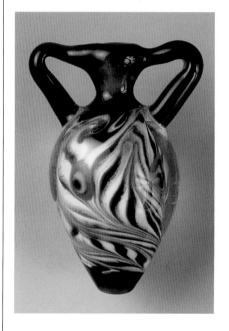

Top: Loren Stump, heavily encased sculptural flower with floral embellishments applied to casing, 4.2 x 2.9 cm

Photograph: Evan Bracken

Bottom: Patricia Sage, vase bead with peacock eye, cased lower portion of vessel, 4.6 cm high

Photograph: Evan Bracken

DICHROIC GLASS

Ah—dichroic glass. You really have to see it for yourself. Because it changes constantly, depending on the angle and lighting you use to view it, no photograph can ever really capture it completely. Dichroic glass can bring eye-popping glitz or just a subtle shimmer to the inside of a bead. How you use it makes all the difference.

What is this high-tech mystery glass? Dichroic glass isn't really new, but it's a fairly recent addition to the art glass community. It's made in a heated vacuum chamber, where aluminum, chromium, silicon, titanium, and zirconium are applied to the glass in varying layers, depending on the colors desired. The thin metallic layers produce completely different colors in reflected and transmitted light. There is also a third "shift" color that results from viewing the glass at an angle, where you can see a bit of both the transmitted and reflected light.

Because the metallic coating has a much higher melting temperature than the glass, the more you heat, stretch, and distort the glass, the more the dichroic layer will break up into isolated spots of color that constantly shift according to your viewing angle.

You can purchase dichroic-coated sheets of glass, which you can cut into strips to use for your beads. Effetre glass rods are also available with a dichroic coating.

Cindy Jenkins, left to right: sheet casing, 1.7 x 1.5 cm; wound casing with grooved surface, 2 x 1.5 cm; full-gather casing, 1.5 x 1.5 cm; encased dichroic glass, 1.8 x 1.2 cm

Photograph: Evan Bracken

Heating and applying dichroic glass is not quite as simple as using other types of glass. If the coating is thin (depending on the color and the manufacturer), it may be sensitive to the flame. You can lose the coating altogether or find yourself left with a gray scum. To prevent these mishaps, expose the dichroic coating to as little direct flame as possible while applying it to your bead. Direct your flame toward the uncoated side as much as possible.

This isn't much of a problem with a clear base because the dichroic coating shines through. With a black base, the coated side *must* be left exposed while it's applied in order for it to be seen at all. Clear dichroic glass is by far the most versatile choice, as you can use it over a core bead of any color, including black.

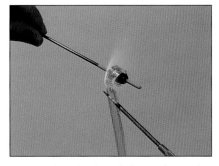

Heat and apply clear dichroic glass with the *coated* side facing the core bead, pressing the glass against the bead with a rake or other tool.

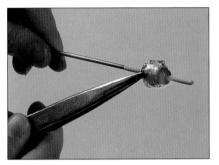

Use a pair of tweezers or another pointed tool to seal the edges of the dichroic glass against the bead. This prevents the coating from rolling up on the edges and being exposed to the flame. The clear glass on the outside protects the dichroic coating from the heat, reduces the chances of scum forming, and helps prevent the coating from disappearing.

HOT TIP

SOME BEADMAKERS PREFER TO USE A VERY COOL FLAME WHEN WORK-ING WITH DICHROIC GLASS.

If you plan to make a simple bead that doesn't require a lot of heating and shaping, you can leave the coating exposed on the surface. For more complicated beads, case the dichroic coating with a transparent color as soon as possible.

SCULPTED BEADS

If you're ready to break away from symmetrical shapes and try sculpting a bit, the easiest place to begin is with a freeform shape.

Make a disk-shaped bead and use a knife or other tool to push in the edges at various places. Try playing with your beads a bit, adding glass here and there, pinching and poking. Once you've become familiar with how the glass responds, move on to more specific shapes.

HEARTS

Start with a fairly simple shape, such as a heart, and think about which direction you'd like the hole to go through the bead. This choice determines how you will build the bead on the mandrel.

For a heart-shaped bead with a vertical hole, start with a thin cylinder. The length of the cylinder will become the height of your heart bead.

To left: Inara Knight (left), dichroic glass sculpted bead, 3.3 x 3.4 cm; Patricia Frantz (right), dichroic tabular bead, 3.7 x 2.5 cm

Photograph: Evan Bracken

Top right: Patricia Frantz (left), dichroic bicone, 4.3 x 1.6 cm; Lorraine Yamaguchi (center), patterned dichroic bicone with dichroic overwrap, 4.3 x 2.2 cm; Patricia Frantz (right), dichroic tabular bead, 3.8 x 3.1 cm

Photograph: Evan Bracken

Bottom: Stevi Belle, *Plumb Bob Asteroid*, dichroic glass and metals, 7.7 x 3 cm

Photograph: Evan Bracken

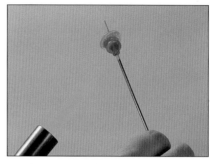

Work toward making the cylinder into a cone by winding some extra glass around the middle and even more around the top. Heat this in your flame until it becomes a true cone. At this point I like to flatten the cone a bit, but that's not a necessity.

Now add some extra glass onto the shoulders of the flattened cone to round them out.

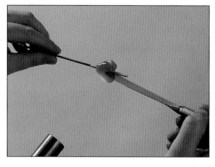

Use your rake, paddle, or knife to put a little crease at the top center of the heart on the back and front. Heat and reshape any parts as needed, until you're satisfied with the overall shape.

If you'd rather have a horizontal hole through the heart, the process is different. Again start with a thin cylinder, but this time its length will become the width of your finished heart.

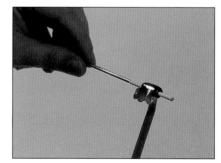

Now add extra bumps of glass near each end of the cylinder on the same side. This will become the top of the heart.

On the opposite side, add about three stripes of glass, one on top of the other. The first one should be centered and a bit shorter than the length of the cylinder. Center the second and make it shorter still. The third should be not much more than a dot in the center. This will form the bottom half of the heart. Using your paddle, flattener, and rake, alternately heat and shape until you have a symmetrical heart.

FLOWER

The easiest way to make a flower bead is to start with a small round core bead and add dots around the equator. To add interest, make the central core one color and the dots another.

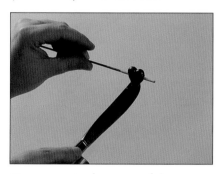

Put a crease in the center of the top on both the front and back to accentuate the valley in the top of the heart.

Heat and pinch each dot with needle-nose pliers to form it into a petal.

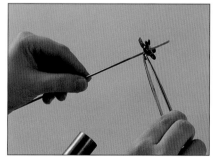

To make leaves, add some green dots on the bottom and pinch them into the appropriate shapes. Pinching creates rounded forms; I like to elongate the leaves by pulling them with tweezers or fine needle-nose pliers. Alternatively, you can use a cold stringer of the same color to pull the heated tips out a bit. Heat just the ends of the leaves and tug at their tips to pull them to a point.

Cindy Jenkins, freeform sculpted bead, 2.7 x 1.8 cm; red horizontal heart, 2 x 2.2 cm; pink vertical heart, 2.3 x 2.3 cm

Photograph: Evan Bracken

Top: Al Janelle, potted flowering plant, 3.5 x 2.5 cm

Photograph: Al Janelle

Center: Peggy Prielozny, sunflower beads, 2 x 2.2 cm

Photograph: Evan Bracken

Bottom: Loren Stump, netsuke mouse, 2.3 x 2.7 cm

Photograph: Evan Bracken

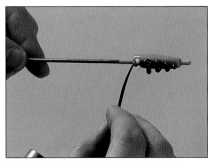

Left: Loren Stump, five-car necklace, 3 x 2.2 (typical car)

Photograph: Evan Bracken

Above: Loren Stump, detail of car

Photograph: Evan Bracken

Once you've made a few of these simple flowers, try making one with two or more rows of petals. Start with a thin green cylinder for a stem and build your flower on top of that.

Apply a series of dots on top of other dots, varying the color on each layer for a two-toned flower.

Cindy Jenkins, single flower, .9 x 2.2 cm; double flower, 2.7 x 2 cm

Photograph: Evan Bracken

HOT TIP

WHEN MAKING TWO-TONED FLOWER PETALS, TRANSPARENT COLORED DOTS APPLIED OVER OPAQUE DOTS CREATE EXTRA DEPTH.

ANIMALS

When making animal beads, the direction you choose to have the mandrel hole run through the bead makes a big difference in the appearance of the finished piece—and how hard the bead will be to make! For your first attempt at an animal bead, make it simple. Normally, working from the mouth to the tail is the easiest.

Wind a cylinder for the body and add dots of hot glass along one side for "scales" and eyes. Let the cylinder itself be both the head and body.

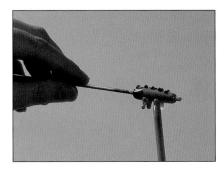

If desired, use a black stringer to add pupils to the eyes. For the mouth, wind the stringer around the head end of the bead, placing it as close as possible to the very edge. You can also add a smile line on each side, if you like.

Using a rod of the same color as the body, add short, stocky posts for the legs. Now bend the ends of the legs into feet with a pair of tweezers.

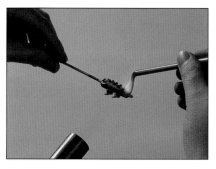

At this point you can add some extra glass to thicken the body, if needed, and apply a curvy tail at the end. Customize your creature with toenail dots, ears, spots, or any details you like.

The longer, thinner, and more elaborate the parts become, the more precise your heat control must be. If you're going to make lots of small, thin appendages on your animals, you need to have a hot kiln (annealer) ready to accept your finished beads. A kiln prevents the thin areas from cooling more quickly than the thicker ones and minimizes the potential for cracking.

HOT TIP

THINK ABOUT THE CONSTRUCTION OF YOUR SCULPTURED BEAD OR SKETCH IT OUT ON PAPER BEFORE YOU START BUILDING IT. DECIDE WHICH STEPS YOU WANT TO DO FIRST AND WHICH SHOULD BE LAST. IN GENERAL, YOU WANT TO GET THE BASIC SHAPE, COLOR, AND DECORATION BUILT BEFORE YOU APPLY FINELY DETAILED APPENDAGES. IF YOU MAKE TINY EARS THAT COME TO PERFECT POINTS BEFORE YOU'VE FINISHED YOUR HIGHEST TEMPERATURE WORK ON THE CORE BEAD, THOSE POINTED LITTLE EARS WILL JUST ROUND UP AND MELT BACK INTO THE BEAD. PLAN YOUR SCULPTURE IN STAGES TO AVOID HAVING TO REDO YOUR DETAIL WORK.

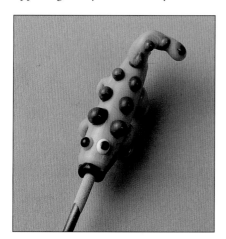

Cindy Jenkins, animal bead, 3.7 x 1.4 cm

Photograph: Evan Bracken

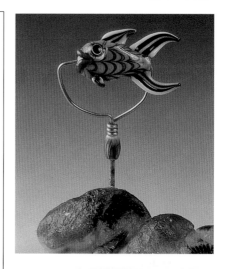

Top left: Jacob Fishman, two red dogs, 3 x 3.5 cm (larger)

Photograph: Evan Bracken

Top right: Phyllis Clarke, two Siamese and one black cat, 4.5 x 3 cm (leaping Siamese)

Photograph: Evan Bracken

Center: Brian Kerkvliet, fish, 4.5 x 2.7 cm, with paté de verre base by Char Eagleton

Photograph: Evan Bracken

Bottom: Al Janelle, pair of white rabbits, 2.9 x 3.8 cm

Photograph: Al Janelle

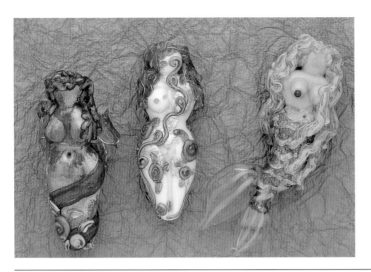

Left: Kimberley Osibin, *The Three Goddesses, Nike, Flora, and Mari,* 2.5 x 7.6 cm (largest)

Photograph: George Post

Above: Al Janelle, quadruple, double, and single lizard beads, 4.4 cm long (largest)

Photograph: Al Janelle

FISH

Fish beads are extremely popular, both with beadmakers and jewelry lovers. To make a fish bead, first build a cylindrical core for the body.

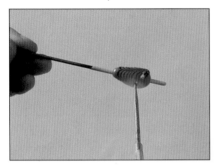

One popular way to decorate fish bodies is to wind a fine spiral trail around the core and rake it in a single direction toward the tail. This both simulates scales and lends a sense of movement and direction to the fish.

Build up the body to the desired size and add glass to selected areas to get the shape you want. Add bulk to the front end for a goldfish-type body, make a symmetrical ball for a blowfish, or use your flatteners to squash a cylinder to make an angel fish.

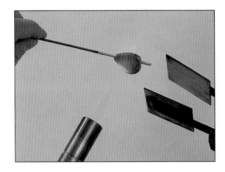

I find that a flattened teardrop-shaped body works well.

Try to shape the body so that the mandrel hole is closer to the fish's back than to its underside. You want the fish to be a little bottom-heavy so that it hangs right side up when strung on a necklace.

Once the body is fully shaped and decorated, begin working on the face.

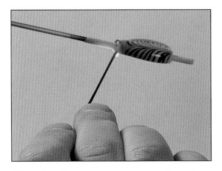

Use a black stringer to wrap a fine circle at the front end of the bead, as

close to the very edge as you can get it. This will create an interior to the mouth. Again using stringer, wrap a fine red line along the edge of the black circle where it joins the body of the bead. This will create lips for your fish. Using a rake, pull the sides of the lips into a grin, if you wish. Don't press too deeply with the rake; the mouth structure is very thin and you can easily dig into the bead separator.

HOT TIP

BECAUSE RED GLASS LOOKS BLACK WHILE IT'S HOT, IT'S DIFFICULT TO SEE THE JOINT BETWEEN RED LIPS AND A BLACK MOUTH UNTIL YOUR BEAD HAS COOLED.

Use a stringer to apply a small dot of white glass on either side of the face, where you want to build the eyes. Using another stringer, completely cover the white with a dot of transparent blue (or whatever transparent color you wish).

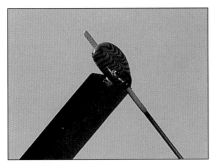

Press the transparent blue with your paddle so that it creates a smooth, even coating. Try to avoid making the eyes too large. Let the eyes cool and add a tiny dot of black in the center with your stringer. If the eyes are too hot when you do this, you may smear the dot and get a blurry streak rather than a fine pupil. Place this black dot carefully—it determines which direction your fish is looking! Melt the black dot completely and flatten the eyes; then let them grow fairly cold.

Now carefully add a small but very hot drop of clear glass right on top of each eye. Round the eyes with your flame, but don't melt them in completely; the clear glass creates a tiny magnifier as well as a nice eyeball shape. Using only the flame to shape the eyes from this point forward will help you keep their shape intact.

Start building the fins much as you did the limbs on your animal bead. Think of where you want them; a fish typically has a large dorsal fin on the back, one or two ventral fins on the underside, and a tail fin that can be single or split into two halves.

Build a series of dots on dots to make small lumps that protrude from the

body at the points where you want the fins to attach. Try varying the color of the layers in the fins, slipping a line of white between transparent colors to create definition. Try putting tiny dots of a bright color at the very tip of the fin bumps to further accent the shape.

Before proceeding, be sure that the fin bumps are thoroughly heated and attached to the body. They must be well adhered, or they can snap off after the fish has cooled. Once you start manipulating the bumps into thin fins, it's difficult to go back and sufficiently reheat the attachment points without losing the detail in the fins.

Once you're confident that they are well attached to the body, use your needle-nose pliers to begin manipulating the fins. (Remember to reheat the entire bead after working on each of the fins.) Start with the ventral fins and pinch a series of impressions into them. While doing the same on the dorsal fin, try to pull it back toward the tail. To simulate movement, give the fin a bit of a ripple along the top. Finally pinch, pull, and shape the tail fin until you're happy with its appearance.

As a final step for this or any sculptured bead, return the bead to the flame and equalize the heat throughout. Remember that the thick body

Top: Brian Kerkvliet, *Lizard Group*, 5.1 cm long (typical)

Photograph: David Scheere

Center: Patricia Sage, *Phoenician*, 7.6 x 5.1 cm

Photograph: Tom Holland

Bottom: Kate Fowle, champagne bottle and glasses, 2.4 cm high (bottle)

Photograph: Evan Bracken

Gina Lambert, black hollow bead with black-and-white twisties and dots, 2 x 2.5 cm; white hollow bead with black-and-white twisties, 1.7 x 2.1 cm

Photograph: Evan Bracken

Gina Lambert, five hollow beads with dots and twisties on outer surfaces, 1.5 x 2.2 cm (typical)

Photograph: Evan Bracken

will be slow to heat and cool, but those thin fins will heat quickly and lose detail. To give the body a chance to heat up again without losing the detail in the fins, briefly pass your fish bead in and out of the flame several times.

HOT  TIP

REMEMBER THOSE SIMPLE CANES YOU MADE BY CASING A GLASS ROD WITH AN OPAQUE COLOR? THEY MAKE PERFECT EYE SLICES FOR YOUR FISH AND ANIMAL BEADS. APPLY AND ENCASE THEM AS YOU DO MILLEFIORI. THIS IS AN EASY WAY TO GET BOTH EYES TO MATCH.

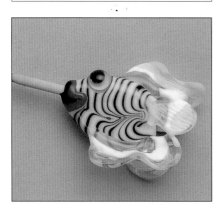

Ed Weisbart, fish bead, 4 x 3.5 cm

Photograph: Evan Bracken

HOLLOW BEADS

A lot of people think that hollow beads have to be mouth-blown. That is one method, but it's also possible to wind a hollow bead right onto your mandrel.

For a simple hollow bead, begin by winding a thin cylinder.

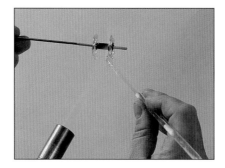

At each end, wind a tall, narrow disk of clear glass. Alternate between the two disks as you're building them so that one doesn't cool too much and crack.

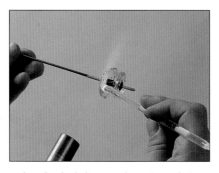

When both disks rise about ½ inch (1.3 cm) from the mandrel, begin gradually closing the gap between them.

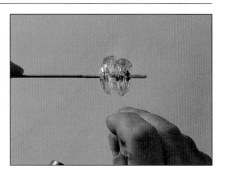

Start winding each layer slightly closer to the opposing disk, until the clear glass meets in the center. Now equalize the heat throughout the whole piece. While you have the bead in the flame, check for gaps between the coils and put a small patch of glass over any that

HOT  TIP

WHEN MAKING HOLLOW BEADS, SOME BEADMAKERS PREFER TO USE TWEEZERS OR PLIERS TO COAX THE TWO DISKS TOWARD EACH OTHER; THEN THEY CRIMP THE EDGES TOGETHER ALL THE WAY AROUND. EXPERIMENT TO SEE WHICH TECH-NIQUE WORKS BEST FOR YOU.

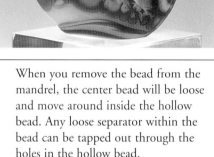

Right: Linda Burnette, hollow bead with flowers on exterior, 1.6 x 2.5 cm

Photograph: Evan Bracken

Far right: Karen Ovington, hollow bead, 2 x 3 cm

Photograph: Tom Van Eynde

you find. You may want to use tweezers to close tiny holes.

Continue to heat the bead until all the clear glass begins to flow together. Once the glass has flowed and the surface sealed, the air inside the bead will start to expand.

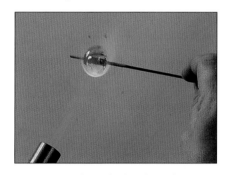

Continue to heat the bead until it becomes completely round. Once it's finished, place the hollow bead in an annealer to cool under controlled conditions.

When making hollow beads, you must be careful not to allow the surface of the bead to touch the mandrel or any part inside the bead. If this happens, the bubble will collapse in on itself, creating a solid bead with a small air bubble on one side rather than a hollow bead. Don't let this discourage you—just try again!

VARIATIONS

Embellish your core bead with some frit, twisties, stripes, dots, or other simple

decorations; then build your hollow bead over the decorated core. The bubble of clear or transparent glass tends to magnify the decorations. For real drama, try this with a dichroic core!

Another option is to decorate the outside of a hollow bead with frit, dots, stripes, twisties, millefiori, or any sort of design that appeals to you. This technique allows you to make large beads that aren't too heavy for earrings or for a necklace having several large beads.

If you really want to impress your friends, make a bead *within* your hollow bead. Wind a small bead and start your disks, leaving a gap of at least ¼ inch (6 mm) on each side of the small center bead. Continue building your hollow bead as before, until it makes a complete bubble over the core bead.

HOT TIP

BE CAREFUL NOT TO GET WATER INSIDE A HOLLOW BEAD WHEN CLEANING IT; IT'S VERY DIFFICULT TO REMOVE ANY SPOTS AND RESIDUE THE WATER MAY LEAVE BEHIND.

When you remove the bead from the mandrel, the center bead will be loose and move around inside the hollow bead. Any loose separator within the bead can be tapped out through the holes in the hollow bead.

BUTTONS

Once you've mastered beadmaking, you may want to try making buttons.

Unlike beads, buttons are usually made by working primarily off your glass rod rather than by winding onto a mandrel. The mandrel comes into play during the final steps, when you're adding a shank to the button.

Make the core of the shank ahead of time by cutting a piece of copper tubing that is about half as long as the expected width of your button. If you're using a ³⁄₃₂-inch (2.4 mm) mandrel, copper tubing that is ⁵⁄₃₂ inch (4 mm) in diameter works well. Place the piece of tubing on a mandrel and set it aside for later.

Begin your button by holding a glass rod so that it's almost vertical, with the tip facing up into the flame. This causes the glass to thicken and spread into a mushroom shape as it melts. Any decoration you wish to add should be done on the top of this surface. Combinations of any and all decorating techniques can be used: dots,

Top: David Vogt, *Space Cat Button*, 2.3 x 1.2 cm
Photograph: Evan Bracken

Center: David Vogt, reverse side of button
Photograph: Evan Bracken

Bottom: Peggy Prielozny, three hollow snail beads, 2 x 1.7 cm (typical)
Photograph: Evan Bracken

stripes, twisties, rosettes, millefiori, casing—the list is endless.

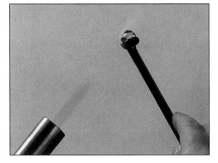

In this example, the top of the button is decorated with a millefiore slice that is embellished with tiny green leaves, then encased with a dot of clear glass.

Tools can be used to help dictate the final shape of the button, and the most useful of these is a button mold, sometimes referred to as a *marble* or *cabochon mold*. You can make buttons without a mold, but since it's important for buttons to be a uniform size, I find the mold indispensable. A button mold is usually a graphite paddle with various sizes of half-round concave wells.

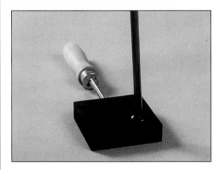

Rolling the hot glass in the wells as you build and decorate your button helps maintain a perfectly smooth dome shape.

Once you're happy with the overall size and appearance of the button, you must attach another glass rod to the front face of the button so that you can complete the back. Generally, a clear rod will work well and not leave a mark on the button's surface, but you may want to match the transfer rod to

a particular color in the middle of your button design.

Heat your transfer rod and marver it into a fairly small point; then heat the center of the top of the button and attach the transfer rod. Holding the button from the front with the transfer rod, concentrate your torch flame on the original rod attached to the back of the button and melt off the rod completely. Don't worry if there is a small bump or burr on the back of the button; this will help hold the copper tubing in place.

Holding the button in one hand, pick up the mandrel and copper tubing in the other.

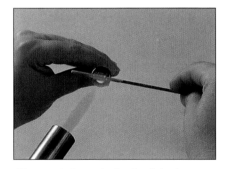

Alternately heat the back of the button and the copper tubing until both are glowing; then press the tubing lengthwise onto the back of the button to make the shank. To secure the shank on the button, wrap a layer of button-colored glass over the tubing. This will prevent the shank from coming loose, and it will cover the rough edges of the tubing, which might tear the thread used to attach the button to a garment.

Above: Dina Hulet, two marbles with millefiori slices, 3.8 cm dia.

Photograph: Patty Hulet

Right: Brian Kerkvliet, six marbles among assorted beads, 6.4 cm dia. (largest)

Photograph: Brian Kerkvliet

MARBLES

From making buttons, it's only a short leap to make a marble. (A marble is basically a double-sided button.) For marble making in the torch, work straight off the glass rod, just as you did for a button. Heat the tip of the rod in the flame, holding it so that it's almost vertical, and let the glass form a ball.

When the back of the button is complete, remove the transfer rod from the front surface. You can remove any little bump or burr that may have been left behind by holding the front of the button in the flame until it looks smooth. This is called *fire-polishing*. Once you're satisfied with its appearance, allow the button to cool slowly, just as you've done with your beads.

If you're not concerned about the appearance of the back of the button and don't want to go to the effort of making your own shank, you can make your button without a shank and simply glue one on later. Knock the completed button off the rod after it's cool, grind off any burrs, and attach a plastic or metal shank. For good adhesion, use a two-part epoxy or silicone glue.

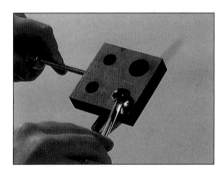

Use a marble mold to shape the first half of the marble. If you want to case your marble after decorating it, make your initial ball of glass fairly small so that you will be able to progress to larger wells in the marble mold as you go along.

Add whatever decorations you prefer—dots, stripes, spiral trails, or any combination of techniques. After adding the desired embellishments, return your marble to the mold to make it perfectly round again.

Encase the marble by winding clear glass over the decorated surface. Again use the mold to make the surface smooth and round.

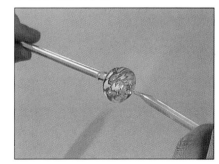

When the first half is done, attach a transfer rod to the center of the finished

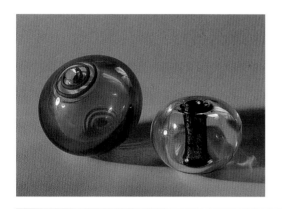

Far left: Brian Kerkvliet (left), blue hollow bead with filigrana ends, 2.1 x 2.5 cm; Char Eagleton (right), clear hollow bead with dichroic core, 1.5 x 2.1 cm

Photograph: Evan Bracken

Left: Peggy Prielozny, four hollow hearts, 1.7 x 1.9 cm (typical)

Photograph: Evan Bracken

side and melt off the original rod. Now build up the second half so that it's comparable to the first. Keep adding glass to the second half of the marble and shaping it in the mold until the glass is nicely rounded.

By now you should be able to roll nearly all of the marble in the mold to shape it.

Once the marble is perfectly round and the size you want it, allow it to cool slightly. Then grasp it with a set of holding fingers. The marble should be slightly cool so that the fingers don't mar the surface, but not so cool that it might crack.

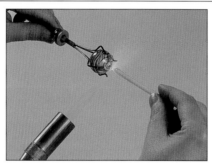

Then melt off the transfer rod. If you find it difficult to fire-polish the remaining burr from the transfer rod while you're holding the marble in the metal fingers, loosen the fingers and let the marble fall into the well of the mold paddle. There you can nudge the marble so that the burr faces into the flame, where it can be smoothed away.

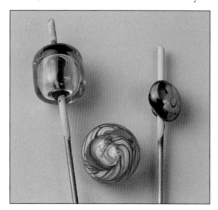

Ed Weisbart (left) hollow bead, 2.1 x 2.1 cm; Cindy Jenkins (center), marble, 2.3 cm dia.; Cindy Jenkins (right), button, 1.7 x 1.1 cm

Photograph: Evan Bracken

The design of your marble can be built into it from the center outward, placed on the outside surface, or both. Since these marbles generally are meant to be viewed rather than actually used, it's okay to leave a textured design on the outside of the marble, if you like.

CORE VESSELS

The core vessel is one of the most ancient of glass containers and surely the most intriguing. Originally core vessels were used to contain precious oils, ointments, perfumes, and even *kohl*—a lead-bearing form of eye makeup used by Egyptian women. Because the art of glassblowing had not yet been discovered, creating a hollow space in the center of a glass object would have required a labor-intensive grinding method. To avoid this, the glass was trailed over a core that could be fairly easily scraped out when the piece was finished, thus producing a vessel or container. Opinions vary widely as to how core vessels originally were made.

There are still several ways of approaching the process today, starting with the core material. The original cores were thought to be made of straw, clay, and dung, but don't worry, we won't be using that method. Many beadmakers favor steel wool as a core material, and I've found very fine steel wool (#3/0 or

4/0) to work best. Unroll a pad of steel wool into a long strip; then tightly wind the strip around the end of a mandrel.

When you've wound enough steel wool for the core of your vessel, use your fingers to continue twisting it in order to tighten and sculpt the shape. If you need to wind some thinner strips of steel wool around the middle or top to widen it, now is the time. The shape of your core will determine the final shape of your vessel.

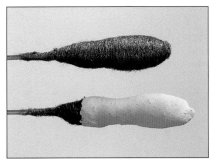

When you're pleased with the overall shape, dip the whole thing into some slightly thinned bead separator. Let it dry. If you're using a flame-dry separator, you may do this in the flame.

Now, using the same thickness of separator that you've been using for general beadmaking, dip the core in the separator and use your fingers to smooth it over the core body. Let it dry again. If the core looks sufficiently covered after drying,

HOT TIP

ROUGHING UP THE MANDREL HELPS THE STEEL WOOL STAY PUT DURING THE INITIAL WINDING PROCESS FOR MAKING A CORE FOR A VESSEL, AND PUTTING THE MANDREL INTO THE CHUCK OF AN ELECTRIC DRILL HELPS TO TWIST THE STEEL WOOL MORE TIGHTLY.

you're ready to go. If not, you may need to add more separator to the sparse areas or even dip the core a third time.

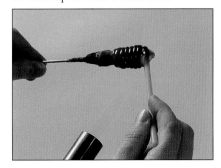

Wind a base layer of glass over the core until it's completely covered. If your torch has a narrow flame, limit the overall length of the core vessel on your first couple of tries. Don't exceed 2 inches (5 cm) in length until you've played with the technique a bit. Make sure to cover the bottom end of the core completely, especially if you plan to put anything into your vessel.

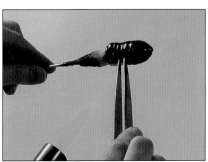

After winding on the glass, use tweezers to pinch closed any gaps.

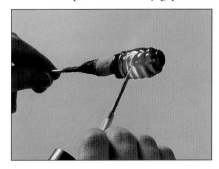

Traditionally, core vessels were decorated with a spiral trail (called a *snake thread*) and combed or feathered. Of course you can decorate your vessel any way you want, using any combination of techniques.

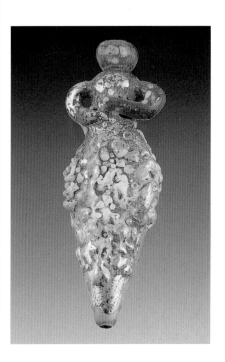

Top: Jessica Bohuš, vase pendant, 3.5 cm high
Photograph: Evan Bracken

Bottom: Stevi Belle, *Goddess Vessel*, 7.9 cm high
Photograph: Jerry Anthony

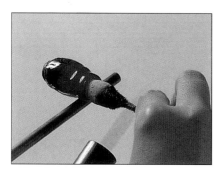

Before adding a foot, a lip, or handles, use your tools to accentuate the desired shape of the vessel. In this example, a metal rod is used to deepen the inward curve near the top.

The foot and lip are added simply by winding some extra glass around the top and bottom of the vessel.

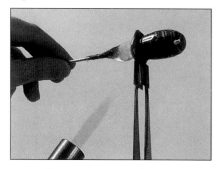

Using flatteners, you can flare the lip or shape it into a spout, if desired.

The final wind can be a different color—a filigrana rod or twistie makes a handsome embellishment. After applying the extra glass at the bottom, stand the vessel on your marver to make sure that the vessel doesn't lean.

Handles are a bit more difficult to master, especially if you want a matched pair. The easiest type of

handle is created by squashing the molten end of a glass rod onto the side of your vessel, pulling the rod out a bit, and melting it off. This makes a simple post-type handle. With this design, it's easy to add a little more glass to one side if the handles look uneven.

Another simple technique is to attach a somewhat longer post to the side of the vessel and heat it evenly. Apply a fairly thick cold stringer across the end of the post and roll it toward the vessel, making a flat spiral. The result is a pleasing earlike handle.

A traditional handle is very elegant but somewhat more difficult. First attach a long post on the side of your vessel where you want the top of the handle to be positioned. Turn your mandrel so that the post hangs straight down from the vessel. Now quickly spot-heat the end of the post and the side of the vessel where you want the bottom of the handle to be attached. (Make sure the post is long enough to reach the full distance, adding more glass if necessary.)

HOT TIP

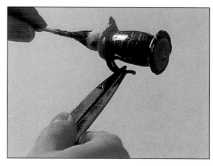

Using a tweezers, grasp the post and bend it into place. (You may need to do this in two or more steps, heating and bending the glass a little at a time.) Spot-heat the handle at the base, making sure that it's well adhered.

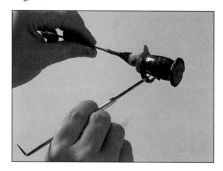

Now use your rake or tungsten pick to shape the handle, running it along the inside edge to smooth the curve. Heat the handle a little at a time so that you don't lose control. Add a second handle, if desired, on the opposite side. When done, you can add extra mass as needed to make the two handles look even.

After it's cool, soak the vessel in water and dig out the steel wool core.

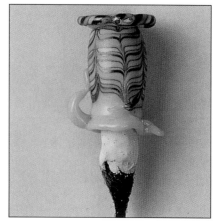

Cindy Jenkins, core vessel, 4.4 cm high

Photograph: Evan Bracken

JEWELRY-MAKING BASICS

Although handmade glass beads are fabulous all by themselves, and the process of making them is lots of fun, most people don't stop there. Stringing your beads into a necklace or assembling them into a pair of earrings is like framing a picture—it gives your beads a beautiful setting for their display.

There are many good books available on stringing beads and assembling them into various types and styles of jewelry, but if you're eager to jump right in and get started making jewelry, here are some of the basic materials, tools, and techniques you'll need.

STRINGING MATERIALS

LEATHER AND DECORATIVE CORDS

Because I like to be able to move my favorite beads to different settings rather than confine them to an elaborately strung piece, I enjoy wearing one or more beads on a knotted length of leather cord. Leather comes in an assortment of colors and sizes, with styles ranging from smooth, round cord to thin strips of rougher-finished leather called thong. No clasp is necessary for this type of necklace, and you can mix and match beads daily or as your whim dictates. For a little more versatility, you can use an adjustable knot, which allows you to change the length of the necklace at will. If you like using leather cord in your designs but prefer to incorporate a clasp, simply attach a pair of crimps or end clamps to the ends of the cord.

Other types of cord include waxed linen and satin cord (also called rattail). These are a little dressier than leather, and both come in a wide variety of colors. Waxed linen cord is fairly thin, flexible, and easily knotted; satin cord is heavier and somewhat stiffer.

BEAD STRING

Another alternative is bead string. When you shop for bead string, you will also find bead thread, which is a lighter (thinner) material that is popular for stringing seed beads and other small beads. Bead thread may work if

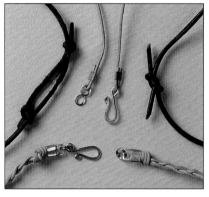

Four ways to finish a necklace made of leather cord are (clockwise starting at top): fold over the ends and apply crimps, tie a square knot, glue and tighten end clamps onto the ends, and tie an adjustable (double) knot.

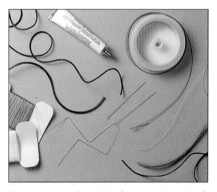

Stringing materials include (first row) two sizes of satin cord, bead tip cement, 49-strand tigertail (with crimp attached at end), 7-strand tigertail, (second row) two colors of bead string, beading needles, two types of leather cord.

your beads are small, but it probably isn't substantial enough for most lampworked beads, since they tend to be fairly heavy. Due to its strength and ability to resist fraying and abrasion, multifilament synthetic string is the most popular. Bead string comes in several colors, but if you're not able to match your beads, choose a color slightly lighter, not darker, than your beads.

Accent beads and necklace by Cindy Jenkins, with focal bead by Inara Knight

Photograph: Evan Bracken

TIGERTAIL

Tigertail is a strong, flexible stainless steel wire coated with nylon. Conventional tigertail consists of seven strands twisted together and tends to be fairly stiff. This can be an advantage if your beads are large and heavy, but a tigertail necklace made of smaller beads can often have an unnatural springiness to it. An updated product consisting of 49 strands has solved this dilemma, and the result is a smooth, flexible coated wire with considerable ease and "drape" to it. Unlike leather or bead string, tigertail can't be knotted; it must be finished at the ends with metal crimp beads.

WIRE AND CHAIN

If you're handy with a pair of pliers, you can fashion your own links to fasten several beads together into necklaces or bracelets. Sterling silver wire is most popular, but gold-plated and gold-filled wire are also available. For those less daring, there are many styles of ready-made chains that can be used to link a few focal beads together into a handsome piece of jewelry.

TOOLS

Few tools are required for making your own jewelry; in addition to having a sharp pair of small scissors, you'll need wire cutters, round-nose pliers, and chain-nose pliers. Purchase a good set of cutters for cutting wire and tigertail. Because tigertail is made of stainless steel, you'll need a pair of wire cutters

made of hardened steel, or repeated use will pit and dull the blades. Round-nose pliers are used to shape wire into loops and other rounded shapes without marring the surface. Chain-nose pliers have jaws that are rounded on the outside and flat on the inside, making them good for crimping things together. Their inside surfaces are smooth, not grooved, so they won't leave marks on your wire or findings.

If you use bead string rather than tigertail or cord to make your jewelry, you'll also need a beading needle. A large-eyed twisted wire needle is best for most projects. The eye is easily threaded, and it closes up neatly when passed through small-holed beads.

If tigertail is your material of choice, you may want to invest in a crimping tool. You can use chain-nose pliers to close a crimp bead onto tigertail, but a crimping tool will do a neater and more secure job.

FINDINGS

There are innumerable findings available that allow you to make just about any piece of jewelry imaginable. You should be able to find what you need at a local bead shop, but if you don't have one near you, try one of the many mail-order jewelry supply companies.

CLASPS

To be able to open and close your necklace or bracelet, you'll need some

Tightening a clamshell bead tip onto a finished strand of beads

type of clasp. Choose one that is both convenient to use and strong enough to hold your beads together. A clasp that's exquisite to behold may require a helper to open and close when you're putting on your necklace. Some type of hook and eye is probably the simplest, and a bar-and-ring clasp is very secure.

HEAD PINS AND EYE PINS

A head pin is a short, straight piece of wire with a flat round head on one end. It's often used to attach a focal bead as a dangle on a bracelet or earring or as a pendant on a necklace. The flat head rests unobtrusively at the bottom of the bead, where it keeps the bead from falling off. Another type of head pin has a decorative round ball in place of the flat head. An eye pin has a loop at one end, which can be attached to anything you want. To use any type of pin, simply add your bead(s), cut the wire to the desired length, and form a loop with the open end.

JUMP RINGS

Simple wire circles called jump rings allow you to connect all the segments of your jewelry together. You can cut and form your own jump rings from wire or buy them in various sizes in both gold and silver. Open a jump ring by pushing one end forward and one end back, not by widening the circle; then close it by pushing the ends in the reverse direction.

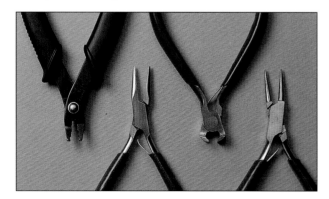

Jewelry-making tools, left to right: crimping tool, chain-nose pliers, wire cutters, round-nose pliers

Some typical findings: (first row) eye pins, hook-and-eye clasp, bar-and-ring clasp, custom-made sterling silver clasp, (second row) barrel end clamp with clasp attached, clamshell bead tips, simple bead tips, head pins (third row) end clamps, crimp beads, (fourth row) two sizes of crimps, jump rings

CRIMP BEADS, CRIMPS & END CLAMPS

Crimp beads are short sections of tiny metal tubing that are primarily used on tigertail to finish the ends. String the tigertail through a crimp bead, then through a clasp. Forming a loop through the clasp, bring the tigertail back through the crimp bead. Tighten the crimp bead onto the tigertail, using a crimping tool or chain-nose pliers, and cut off the excess tigertail. For extra security in case the crimp bead works loose, leave an extra ¾ inch (2 cm) of tigertail at the end to run back through your beads to help hold them in place.

Crimps and end clamps are metal findings used to finish the ends of leather and satin cords. They come in a variety of styles and sizes to fit single or multiple cords. When using them, it's advisable to apply a dab of flexible white craft glue to the ends of the cord before tightening the crimps.

BEAD TIPS

Used to finish jewelry made with bead string or thread, bead tips come in two styles: simple and clamshell. Simple bead tips consist of a round metal cup with a small hole in the center and a metal hook attached to one edge. Clamshell bead tips have two metal cups, which are closed over the knot to hide it completely.

With the hook facing outward, thread a bead tip onto your finished strand of beads; then tie the end of your string so that the knot fits neatly into the cup of the bead tip. Apply a dab of bead tip cement to the knot to secure it and if you're using a clamshell bead tip, close the two cups with the chain-nose pliers. Then pass the hook through your clasp and close it into a loop.

EARRINGS, PINS, & OTHER FINDINGS

For those with pierced ears, French wires, kidney wires, and posts all provide good opportunities for displaying your favorite beads. Screw-backs and clips are also available and may be the better choice for heavier beads.

If your desire is to make something to wear on a jacket or sweater, you can find dozens of styles of preshaped wire pins to which you can add your beads. Silver is probably the most popular, but you can find some designs in dazzling colors as well. Preshaped wire bracelets that are suitable for adding beads are also available.

In addition to the selected findings discussed here, there are many, many more that you may find useful in your jewelry designs.

GLUE

A small dab of glue often can make all the difference between years of wearing pleasure and the dismay of having to pick up your beads from around your feet. If you use bead string, apply some bead tip cement to each knot before closing it into a bead tip; otherwise, your knot is likely to unravel over time. For necklaces made of leather or cord, use a white craft glue that remains flexible after drying. Flexibility is important to prevent the glue from cracking and coming loose with wear.

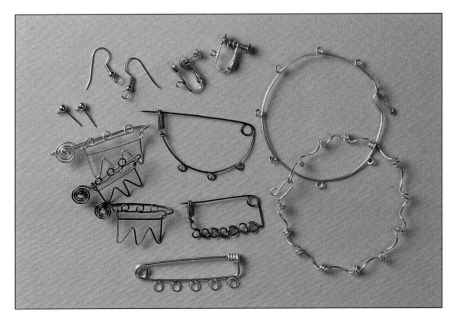

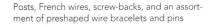

Posts, French wires, screw-backs, and an assortment of preshaped wire bracelets and pins

107

THE NATURE OF GLASS

It's important to understand the basic characteristics of glass so that you'll know what to expect of it. If you know how to treat glass correctly, it will yield remarkably beautiful results. Mistreat it, and glass will find a way to get even with you.

TYPES OF GLASS

The most common material you will use to make beads is soft glass, also called *soda-lime* glass. Its main ingredient is silica, but the mixture also contains calcium and sodium. Calcium acts as a stabilizer and makes the glass durable; sodium is a flux, which lowers the melting temperature of silica. Nearly 90 percent of all glass manufactured is soda-lime. Because of its high expansion, it is easily manipulated when hot. Soda-lime glass is also relatively low in cost.

Borosilicate glass was developed by the Corning Glass Works for use in scientific laboratory equipment. This harder glass is more resistant to thermal shock and chemical attack than soda-lime glass, and it is also stronger. Sold under the trade name *Pyrex,* borosilicate glass is stiffer than soda-lime glass and less easy to manipulate when it's hot. It is low in expansion and somewhat more expensive than soft glass.

WORKING RANGE

Glass has no definite melting or freezing point. Instead, as you heat it, glass gradually softens until it becomes liquid. As it cools, it becomes increasingly stiff.

In a crystalline solid, the atoms are held together by identical bonds and arranged in a specific repeating pattern.

When the melting temperature is reached, all of the bonds break at once and the solid becomes a liquid. The atoms in glass are randomly arranged, and the bonds that hold them together are not identical. Because the bonds break at different temperatures, only a small percentage may be broken at a lower temperature. As you increase the temperature, more and more bonds break, and the glass becomes increasingly fluid.

The chart below describes the relative stiffness of glass at different temperatures.

COMPATIBILITY

Like most materials, glass expands as you heat it and contracts as you cool it. The rate at which it expands can be measured and assigned a number. This number is called the *linear coefficient of expansion* (*LCOE* or, more commonly, *COE).* The COE is a unit of length per degree of temperature. These numbers are extremely small (lots of 0s behind a decimal point), and for greater ease of understanding, the COE is normally stated in whole numbers. For example, Effetre's COE is 104 (it actually varies from 104 to 108), Bullseye and Uroboros tested-compatible glass have a COE of 90, ordinary window glass is approximately 86, and borosilicate (Pyrex) glass is approximately 32.

Generally the COE of any two types of glass that you want to mix together should be as close as possible. Since beads are usually fairly small, you have a little more leeway than you do with other hot-glass applications. Normally glass must be within a single expansion point to be compatible, but glass within two or three expansion points of each

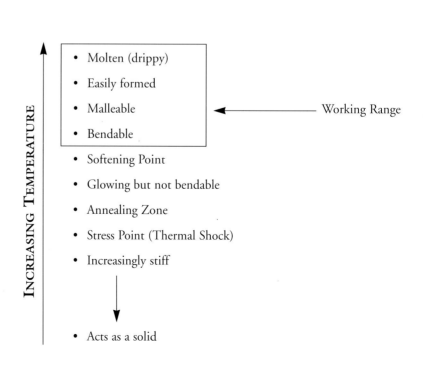

INCREASING TEMPERATURE

- Molten (drippy)
- Easily formed
- Malleable
- Bendable

← Working Range

- Softening Point
- Glowing but not bendable
- Annealing Zone
- Stress Point (Thermal Shock)
- Increasingly stiff
- Acts as a solid

other should work for making beads. For large projects, a difference of more than one point may be unacceptable.

Incompatible glass will mix and work together fine during the heating process because everything is fluid. It's only when you attempt to return the glass to room temperature that the trouble starts. When one section of your bead shrinks more than another, the result is stress. If this stress exceeds the strength of the glass, your bead will break. Depending upon the severity of the stress, the piece may hold together for several years before breaking, or it may blow apart immediately. A sudden temperature change or impact with something else may be the straw that breaks the bead. *With a 14-point difference in COEs, you should never add Effetre millefiori to Bullseye or Uroboros tested-compatible glass, nor should you apply Bullseye stringer to your Effetre beads.* And don't even think about mixing Pyrex with either Bullseye or Effetre—you'd essentially be making little "bombs!"

THERMAL SHOCK

Another type of stress is called *thermal shock*. Breakage as a result of thermal shock occurs when you heat or cool a bead too rapidly. (Think about what happens when you drop an ice cube into hot water—it breaks *before* it melts!) Has the end of your glass rod ever snapped off because you heated it too quickly? That's thermal shock. If you leave your freshly made bead out in the open air, it will probably split before the outside surface is cool enough to touch.

ANNEALING

Okay, you made sure all the glass you're using had the same COE, and you didn't shock the glass during the heating or cooling phases, but a day later your prize bead broke into two pieces. What's going on here?

We need to discuss *annealing*.

Annealing is a word frequently associated with hot-glass working, but what does it mean? Remember the old saying, "Look that up in your Funk and Wagnall's?" (If you do, I know how old you are.) Well I *did* look it up in my Funk and Wagnall's, and the definition is "to toughen something formerly brittle by heating and then *slow* cooling" or "to render enduring." We all want our pieces to endure. Whether you sell your beads or give them as gifts, you don't want them coming back broken.

Keep those two words "slow cooling" in mind. What actually happens when you cool glass quickly? As you know, glass shrinks and becomes rigid as it cools. When cooled rapidly, the outside of the glass object shrinks and hardens first. Meanwhile, the center of the glass, which remains hot, continues to shrink and pull against the hardened exterior. This creates tension or stress between the two areas, and if the stress is severe enough, it will pull the glass apart. The result is a cracked or a completely broken bead.

You can slow the cooling process by placing your beads into a *kiln*. A kiln is a brick-lined or fiber-insulated "oven" that is designed to produce and retain high temperatures. To be effective, a kiln must include a *pyrometer* (a high-temperature thermometer to read the internal temperature of the kiln) and some means to control the power level. The simplest control device is an *infinite-control switch*, which allows you to set the temperature as "warmer" or "cooler" but won't let you specify a particular temperature. With an infinite-control switch on your kiln, you will need to adjust the dial between the high and low settings to make the temperature increase, hold steady, or come down at the proper rate. Computerized controllers are available that can be programmed to run the entire cycle for

you; they tend to be expensive but are well worth the money.

Maintaining the kiln for an hour at the annealing temperature (968°F/520°C for Effetre) should be more than sufficient to anneal your beads. Generally 30 minutes is plenty. A range of 950° to 1000°F (510° to 538°C) is acceptable for annealing most soft glass beads.

HOT TIP

YOU CAN'T *OVER*-ANNEAL GLASS, SO DON'T WORRY ABOUT LETTING YOUR BEADS SOAK ALL DAY WHILE YOU WORK. ONLY IF YOUR KILN IS SET TOO HIGH AND THE GLASS STARTS TO DEFORM WILL YOU HAVE A PROBLEM.

Once you've "soaked" the beads at the annealing temperature, you can start lowering the heat. If you're working in a brick kiln, you can simply turn it off because the bricks retain their heat for a long period of time. If you're working with a fiber-insulated kiln (which heats and cools much faster), spend about 1½ hours reducing the temperature to 600°F (315°C). Then turn off the kiln. Don't remove the beads until the kiln is back to room temperature. If you open the kiln too early, you may still break your annealed beads by exposing them to thermal shock.

Putting your hot beads (still on their mandrels) directly into a preheated kiln as soon as you finish making them is the best way to make sure they will survive. If that isn't possible, you can anneal the beads later (off their mandrels) by putting them in a kiln and slowly bringing it up to the annealing temperature, soaking, and then cooling as previously described.

TROUBLESHOOTING

- **Bead separator pulls off immediately as you touch the hot glass to the mandrel**

Either the tip of the hot glass or the mandrel (or both) wasn't quite hot enough for them to stick together. If the glass attaches only partially, the bead separator will loosen when you start to rotate the mandrel. If the end of your glass rod has bead separator clinging to it, break off that portion; you don't want bead separator wrapped into your next bead.

- **Hot glass doesn't stick to the mandrel at all**

Either you forgot to heat the mandrel, or you heated it too briefly. Another possibility is that the tip of your glass rod wasn't hot enough.

- **The surface of your bead has separator stuck to it**

If you continue rotating the mandrel after you've exhausted all your hot glass, you'll force the cold glass to try to bend. This tugging can pull the separator from the mandrel, and the separator may end up on the surface of your bead.

Marvering too vigorously can have the same effect. Squashing the bead on the marver with too much pressure occasionally loosens the bead separator. This usually happens when you're working with glass that's too cold. If you're marvering just the ends of your bead to make them even, be careful not to push the separator into your bead.

If you find that you do have separator on your bead, you can salvage it by soaking your bead in a glass etching solution. This may take several minutes or up to a couple of hours, depending on how deeply the separator has penetrated into the glass. Etching will impart a satin or

matte finish to your bead that is quite attractive; you may want to do this to some of your beads just for the effect.

- **You don't have enough hot glass to go all the way around the mandrel**

The two most common mistakes for beginning beadmakers are not keeping the tip of the glass rod hot enough and not touching the hot tip of the glass rod to the mandrel. By touching the glass rod to the mandrel too far back from the hot tip, you're almost certain not to have enough glass to wind all the way around the mandrel.

- **Murky or gray beads**

If you're using a single-fuel torch, try working higher in the flame. If that doesn't solve the problem, turn your flame down a bit and try again. With an oxygen-propane system, either reduce the fuel or increase the oxygen in the flame.

- **Bead is textured or has blanket stuck to it**

Your bead was put away while it was still too hot. I call these "Santa beads" because they often look as if they have little white beards. The fiber can be removed, but the texture is permanent.

- **Sharp pointed ends on your bead**

Glass tends to ball up as you heat it. If your entire bead is too thin or irregular in thickness near its ends, the center of your bead will thicken as you heat it by pulling the glass away from the ends. To prevent this, marver your bead to push the center back toward the ends and recess the hole. Another option is to wind the center a little thicker so that it won't have to "steal" glass from the ends.

- **Really stubborn beads that won't come off the mandrel**

Prevention is the key here; if you have this problem often, pay more attention to all of the basic techniques. Is your separator coating too thin, too thick, scratched, or chipped? If you're not using flame-dry separator, are your mandrels dry before you start working? Do you find yourself trying to force cold glass to wind? Did you overheat the mandrel? (There's no need to preheat the mandrel so that it's glowing brightly; this exhausts the separator and makes it fail). Did you manipulate the bead too roughly with your tools? Did you squash it too firmly when you tried to flatten it? These are all possible explanations for why your bead won't release from the mandrel.

- **Bead breaks or cracks after cooling**

Either the bead was put away too cold, or it was shaped in such a way that the sides were too thin. Your bead should be at least as thick as the mandrel all the way around.

If you're making beads larger than ½ inch (1.3 cm) in diameter, they should be put in a kiln at approximately 950° to 1000°F (510° to 540°C) and then slowly cooled. When making larger beads, leave the hot bead still on the mandrel and put it directly into a kiln that is holding at 950° to 1000°F. Alternatively, after the bead has cooled in the blanket and been removed from the mandrel, it can be put into a cold kiln and slowly brought up to 950° to 1000°F for annealing (slow cooling).

Another reason for a bead to break after cooling is that you mixed two or more types of incompatible glass together.

CONTRIBUTING ARTISTS

Kimberley Adams
Kimberley Adams Handmade
Glass Bead Jewelry
Fletcher, North Carolina

Michael Barley
Hori Designs
Sequim, Washington

Stevi Belle
Winged Woman Creations
Taylorville, Illinois

Jessica Bohuš
Glenn, Michigan

Tom Boylan
Mendocino, California

Ellie Burke
Milwaukee, Wisconsin

Linda Burnette
Fantasy Beads
Mesa, Arizona

Jana Burnham
Springfield, Illinois

Phyllis Clarke
Glimmerglass
Spring Valley, California

Cay Dickey
Cay of CA
Oceanside, California

Pam Dugger
Hollywood, Florida

Char Eagleton
Eagleton Glass
Mt. Carroll, Illinois

Sue Richers Elgar
Hot Beads
Joliet, Illinois

Leah Fairbanks
Gardens of Glass
San Rafael, California

Jacob Fishman
Lightwriters
Winnetka, Illinois

Kate Fowle
Kate Fowle Lampworked Beads
Washington, D.C.

Patricia Frantz
Frantz Bead Company
Shelton, Washington

Bernadette Fuentes
Arlington, Texas

Angela Green
La Petite Fleur Glass Studio
Oakland, California

G. G. Havens
Stained Glass Haven
Grand Haven, Michigan

Patricia Sage Holland
Beadmakers Holland & Sage
Mountain View, Arkansas

Tom Holland
Beadmakers Holland & Sage
Mountain View, Arkansas

Dinah Hulet
Hulet Glass
McKinleyville, California

Al Janelle
Ambeadextrous
Austin, Texas

Brian Kerkvliet
Gossamer Glass
Bellingham, Washington

Mary Klotz
Forestheart Studio
Woodsboro, Maryland

Inara Knight
Twilight Fire
Lutherville, Maryland

Gina Lambert
Queen Beads
Chicago, Illinois

Kristina Logan
Portsmouth, New Hampshire

Bernadette Mahfood
Hot Flash Designs
St. Charles, Minnesota

Michael Max
Modern Alchemy
Seattle, Washington

Jacqueline Mixon
JM Design
Saugus, California

Kelly Niemann
Planets Jewelry
Kalamazoo, Michigan

Carolyn Noga
That's the Bead
Fox Lake, Illinois

Liz Ormes
Liz Ormes Designs in Glass
Monroe, Louisiana

Kristen Frantzen Orr
Mesa, Arizona

Kimberley Osibin
Gaea Glass Works
San Rafael, California

Karen Ovington
Ovington Glass Studio
Evanston, Illinois

Nancy Pilgrim
Fantasy Beads
Mesa, Arizona

Peggy Prielozny
Glass Gardens
Morton Grove,Illinois

Isis Pearl Ray
Raven's Dream
Carnation, Washington

René Roberts
Sebastopol, California

Donna Sauers
Western Springs, Illinois

Don Schneider
Don Schneider Handcrafted Glass
Plymouth, Michigan

Lavana Shurtliff
Lavana Shurtliff Jewelry Design
Mt. Pleasant, Michigan

Susan Simonds
Lakewood, Colorado

James Smircich
San Francisco, California

Loren Stump
Adventure in Glass
Elk Grove, California

Heather Trimlett
La Mesa, California

Scott Turnbull
Zebra Glass
New Russia, New York

David Vogt
Desert Fire Art Glass
Chandler, Arizona

Pati Walton
Pati Walton Lampworked Beads
Highlands Ranch, Colorado

Audrie Wiesenfelder
Skokie, Illinois

Lorraine Yamaguchi
Fusion Products International
Laguna Niguel, California

Barbara Thomas-Yerace
Creative Glasswear
Saline, Michigan

Alice Foster-Zimmerman
ASG Studio
Glendale, Arizona

ACKNOWLEDGMENTS

I would like to thank the many people who contributed their ideas, techniques, advice, and/or big chunks of their time to the effort.

Ed Weisbart, who did the most work and got the worst assignments.

Laura C. Anderson, who read and gave input on the roughest drafts and was always willing to help out in a pinch.

Kate Fowle, who is a font of information and a continuing source of inspiration.

Tom Holland and **Patricia Sage**, who are both wonderful instructors and generous with their extensive knowledge.

Dinah and **Patty Hulet**—I'm so glad I got to take your first (and last) class. I hope it wasn't something I did.

Liz Ormes—a fabulous lampworker, technical advisor, and phone friend who has a great sense of humor.

Tom and **Barb Deibel**, who made sure I got professional photography.

And my muse, **Barb Duro**. (This is all your fault.)

The editor wishes to thank **Kim Adams**, who generously opened her studio to our camera; **Barry Olen**, the owner of Beads and Beyond in Asheville, North Carolina, for lending us tools, findings, and his expertise; Gary Newlin, the owner of A Touch of Glass in Asheville, North Carolina, for providing the perfect background for beadmaking tools; and **Evan Bracken**, whose skillful hand and eye produced hundreds of beautiful photographs for this book.

INDEX